All Right Now!

Free, 1970

1970s Newcastle

Memories from people who were there

Edited by Anna Flowers and Vanessa Histon

Tyne Bridge Publishing

Tyne Bridge Publishing and Newcastle Libraries sincerely thank all our contributors, who gave so generously of their time, memories, photographs, and memorabilia. This book is by you, and for you. We were not able to include everything that was sent to us, and we apologise to those whose memories we could not fit in, but we hope that the following pages give an authentic flavour of what mattered to the people of Newcastle in the 1970s. If it isn't here, then you didn't tell us about it.

Special thanks to ncjMedia and Tyne & Wear Archives and Museums for permission to reproduce their evocative photographs. Our grateful thanks also to Rik Walton (www.rikwalton.com) for his photographs of the 1970s music scene; and to retired journalist and broadcaster Dick Godfrey for writing the introduction.

Illustrations from 1970s publications *Out Now*, *Muther Grumble* (www.muthergrumble.com), and *Tyneside Street Press* in our collection were invaluable additions to the book, along with those from *Newcastle Life* and *Newcastle University Courier*. Photographs by 1970s students Dennis Astridge and Phil Ireson were enormously helpful, and an unexpected bonus.

Unless otherwise indicated illustrations are from the collections of, and are copyright of, Newcastle Libraries.

Our grateful thanks also to our printers Elanders UK Ltd for all their support in the production of this book.

Cover design by Stadt

The views expressed in *All Right Now!* are solely those of the contributors and in no way reflect the views of Tyne Bridge Publishing or the Council of the City of Newcastle upon Tyne.

Opposite, Byker, May 1975.

Haymarket, Newcastle, September 1970.

Contents

Colour sections are inserted after pages 24 and 120

Years May Come, Years May Go

Hermans Hermits, 1969

Newcastle in the 1970s

For the young in their flares and bold prints, gyrating in the shards of light thrown out by a spinning mirror ball to the sounds of Abba, the Bee Gees and Mud, it was the Disco Decade and a load of fun. Everything new was good and highly desirable. And there was a lot of the new around. One of the new digital watches was a 'must have'. And, of course, the snazzy Sony Walkman. Colour TV was increasingly common. Still, there were plenty of jobs so money shouldn't be a problem.

For their parents, there were different concerns. When would they stop mentally converting the new decimal currency, introduced when the decade was barely a year old, back into the comforting familiarity of pounds, shillings and pence? What were the implications of Britain's membership of the European Economic Community that new Tory PM Edward Heath had negotiated in 1970? What could be done about the increasing and apparently destructive power of the trades unions? What if the experts were right and the oil supply from the Middle East was halted?

Such transformation and the worrying arrival of the unfamiliar was the theme of the decade dismissed negatively by one disapproving social historian as 'nasty, brutish and long'.

Change can certainly appear like that and change there was in plenty. Its impact on Tyneside is vividly summed up by a film that, for a time, made a cockney the unlikely voice of Newcastle. Michael Caine was the eponymous hero of *Get Carter* which was released in 1971. The Newcastle it portrayed had not changed much in generations. Thousands of us lived in tightly-packed nineteenth-century terraces. Cars and buses ran on roads that had barely altered in a century. Pubs were the smoke-filled preserves of men who wore caps and spoke fondly of football, whippets and leeks.

But change was in the air which is what had attracted *Get Carter*'s producer Michael Klinger. 'Newcastle is in an incredible state of transition at present, changing from the old to the new,' he said when he arrived for filming. 'Buildings are being demolished and new ones are going up all over the place.' Seen now, *Get Carter* is a either a nostalgic trip down memory lane or a glimpse into the strange world occupied by your parents. The 1970s were to change Newcastle and Tyneside like no other era.

Opposite, the Quayside Sunday Market, 14 September, 1973.

With hindsight, it is possible to see the decade as finally producing much that the 1960s had merely hinted at. If that time of bells, beads and Beatles was the gestation of a new Britain, the 1970s saw its birth. The gestation including laying plans for the transformation of Newcastle's urban landscape. Planners decided to separate the increasing number of vehicles from pedestrians by constructing elevated walkways. So 1970 saw the official opening of Sir Basil Spence's Central Library, which squatted at the centre of a network of aerial walkways stretching from Northumberland Street to Manors alongside the almost immediately unloved newly-created John Dobson Street.

Until the new decade, the A1 ran slap through the city centre along Northumberland Street. This changed when what was then called the Central Motorway East was opened to traffic in 1975, though the full extent of the planned motorway system was never to be completed. And in a development that sums up the progress versus brutal paradox, two sides of the most elegant square in the centre of Newcastle were demolished. 1976 saw the opening of Eldon Square Shopping Centre. The US-style shopping mall had arrived in the UK.

Underfoot things were also stirring. It had been decided to give Tyneside a new 'light railway' or tram system. To serve the region's capital, it had to go underground. Tunnelling work began in 1974. Much of this change was the responsibility of a man whose rise to power in the 1960s was matched by his rapid decline in the following decade. T. Dan Smith had risen through the ranks of the Labour Party to become council leader, national figure, economic planning chief and an extraordinary visionary with the power to have his schemes put into action. He had talked of making Newcastle the 'Brasilia of the North', inviting comparison with a place of which few of the people who elected him had heard.

Old terraces occupied by the 'huddled masses' were ripped down, often to be replaced by gaunt tower blocks that offered homes, but little else. An exception was the highly innovative Byker Wall, which attracted international attention.

Smith himself summed his approach in verse:

From Cruddas Park to Rye Hill
We are determined, have the will
That horrid slums we shall erase
With surgeon's knife and then replace.

But even as the 1970s got underway and the vision of the future he espoused began to become a reality, Smith was poised at the edge of an almighty drop. In Yorkshire in 1973, Yorkshire-based developer and builder John Poulson was involved in bankruptcy proceedings. Evidence threw up the

December 1971, and a familiar Christmas display of reindeer with an unfamiliar glimpse of Percy Street from Blackett Street across the empty space where the west side of Eldon Square had been demolished. The north side would soon follow. The 1970s would see many familiar Newcastle landmarks vanish. There were plans, later abandoned, to move the War Memorial to the Civic Centre.

name of a public relations company owned by T. Dan Smith. It was alleged that money paid by Poulson had been used to buy influence that led to the developer being awarded lucrative contracts. Smith was arrested and pleaded guilty to charges of corruption. He served three years in jail.

The political framework in which Smith flourished wasn't immune from the winds of change. 1974 saw the creation of a new tier of local government with the inception of Tyne and Wear Metropolitan County Council which took over a number of functions that had hitherto been the preserve of District Councils.

But it was the impact of new technology that attracted most interest. It was vividly summed up by Harold Wilson who became Prime Minister of the Labour government that took control in 1974. He talked in beguiling terms of the 'white heat of the new technology' which his administration was to encourage. But the circumstances of Wilson's victory were to cast a long shadow on the 1970s and help shape its legacy as much as the music and new-fangled possessions.

Early that year, Britain's miners had gone on strike for the second time in two years. The first had resulted in Conservative Prime Minister Edward Heath imposing a three-day working week to conserve fuel supplies. A sharp hike in the price of oil hadn't helped matters. The threat of a severe shortage led to the prospect of petrol rationing. Vouchers were issued, but in the end not needed.

In 1974, Edward Heath, faced with more miners' action, called a General Election. 'Who rules Britain?' he challenged. 'Not you,' came the gleeful reply as Harold Wilson's Labour Party won.

Change continued. In 1975, supplies of North Sea oil began to come ashore. The first mass-produced personal computer appeared. Britain's first test tube baby was born. For the young, the sparkly outfits of glam-rock were replaced by the torn jeans, safety pin-adorned jackets and jarring, discordant anarchy of punk rock.

The music matched the times. The 1970s were to end in a manner that came to over-shadow the progress. A series of public sector strikes became the Winter of Discontent of 1978. Rubbish was uncollected. The nation seemed on the verge of chaos.

The reaction came the following May with the election of a new Tory government. A period that had seen distinct improvements for women from the implementation of the Sex Discrimination Act to the right to have the pre-fix 'Ms' on passports produced the country's first female Prime Minister. And Margaret Thatcher was determined to bury the 1970s.

Dick Godfrey

Out with the old, in with the new. Lord Mayor, Councillor Iris Margaret Steedman, the Lady Mayoress, and workmen, celebrate the topping out of the new building that replaced the Old Town Hall between the Groat Market and the Cloth Market, 24 June 1975.

Scotswood Road, New Year's Day, 1975.

Teach your Children

Crosby, Stills, Nash and Young, 1970

Schoolkids

Fights and stripes at Walbottle

I started secondary school in 1971 at Walbottle West. I was a little worried on the first day as the older kids said everyone was shoved down the toilets and the teachers were tough. During the power cuts we shared classrooms in the local grammar school and were amazed to find the grammar kids left their books, pens and supplies in their desks. Needless to say the good stuff disappeared sharpish.

Uniforms were the norm but we wore what was in fashion as long as it matched the colours of the school uniform. Maybe Levi's Sta-Prest instead of generic school pants, switch the tie and wear a gabardine blazer instead of the ugly heavy wool school blazer.

In the early 1970s we carried haversacks – mine was handed down from an older brother – covered in writing. We would throw them at each other over the cloakroom racks at school. I remember the first trainers appearing around the early 1970s.

We were beaten at school. PE teachers used their gym shoes across the backside but the Headmaster had a leather strap that he used often, one lash for minor offences, then two or four. The dreaded six of the best was for serious stuff like fighting. Used correctly and with force it could cause a decent amount of pain to your hands which you were allowed to alternate between lashes.

Often getting six of the best resulted in red dots on your finger tips that we attributed to burst blood vessels. This treatment eventually stopped, probably banned, to be replaced by detention which was easy to handle but lasted longer.

Dale Toothill

Heaton Riot Girls

After the Sex Discrimination Act was passed in 1975 the headmaster at Heaton Comprehensive School decided that girls could from then on be caned or strapped just like the boys. Simon Donald saw what happened when 200 girls staged a protest on the Heaton playing field.

After a swimming lesson at a nearby pool, our bus pulled up back at the school. A large crowd had gathered on the front field. It consisted mainly of older girls, probably fifth formers, some lads of the same age and parents, mainly women, who were at the front. They chanted 'Haway the lads!' and I, in my innocence, assumed it was some sort of football-related gathering … [a teacher chased a boy into the crowd and] I watched in horror as the fists of unseen assailants rained down into the area where the teacher had disappeared from sight.

Simon Donald (extract from 'Him off the Viz', 2010)

Newton Road, Heaton, early 1970s.

On 8 January 1976 Newcastle Evening Chronicle reported 'Schoolgirls go on the rampage' after 200 girls had staged a 'women's lib' protest against the use of the cane for both sexes at Heaton School. The local and then the national newspapers played down the violence but reports went on for days. One boy was arrested, and several boys and 'uncouth and nasty' (Daily Telegraph) girls were suspended.

The school team

As the 1970s began I entered the fourth year, my last at Welbeck Road, with only one thought filling my head: I was going to play for the school team!

I was so proud when I got that kit, you'd have thought they'd given me a World Cup Winner's medal. Royal blue shorts, cotton of course, none of your nylon. White socks, really tight, woollen, that you had to stretch to get on and the most peculiar white cotton v-neck tops, sort of gathered at the waist, unlike any football shirt I've seen before or since, but I got one. It was mine.

Our first game was a friendly against St Peter's School at the end of the third year, just before we broke up for the summer holidays. Nobody had heard of St Peter's School, but one of our old classmates, 'Podger' Holmes was in their team. As we pulled on those shirts we all felt so special. Mark

Heaton Station, mid-1970s, the start of many a summer trip to the coast.

Noble, Titchy Holland, Bella, Noddy, Spelk, my Best Friend Jimmy Brady, I can remember them all even though I haven't seem most of them for almost forty years. All smiling, all filled with pride, each of us realising in the way that only a ten-year-old can that in our own little world in the East End of Newcastle it was our time.

We played on the top pitch on the old Welbeck Road school field and we didn't have nets but it didn't matter when that size 4 leather football dropped in front of me, possibly all of eight yards out, I hit it with all the power my ten-year-old right foot could muster and it sailed between the posts. I was instantly buried beneath my team mates. It didn't matter that we eventually drew 1-1, that Craig Ward would go on to score more goals than me, that Tatty would play for Newcastle Boys, or that Noddy would be made Captain. When it had come to our turn, I had scored first our first goal and this little lad's chest was bursting with pride.

Robin Sword

The school holidays

In the 1970s many people spent summer holidays on deckchairs down the coast at Whitley Bay, Cullercoats or Tynemouth. Package holidays in Spain were still out of reach for most. You kept your eye on the weather forecast and at the merest hint of summer there was a packed lunch with sandwiches and juice and a flask of tea to carry onto a packed train at Heaton Station. During the summer we also went to the Exhibition Park trade show to get all the freebies and to see the Red Devils parachuting team and the White Helmets motorcycle team.

Brian Thompson

A little boy unwraps his picnic on the Whitley Bay sands, early 1970s.

Adventure play in Hodgy Park

In March 1978, I became playworker at Hodgkin Park Adventure Playground. Most of the children came from the nearby Delaval Estate, Scotswood and Benwell Grange. We soon started to build wooden structures and get equipment for the new building, which was so small we called it the hut.

Money and jobs were in short supply at that time and the adventure playground gave the children a place to go that was safe, secure, and free. With excitement there was always some risk, but in the adventure playground this was controlled. However, there were a few unforeseen incidents.

We had scrounged some big tyres and used them in the structures, but we had some left over. Before we could stop them, we realised that some of the older lads had started to roll the tyres down the hill towards Whitehouse Road ... and a car was travelling along the road at the same speed as the tyres!

Hodgkin Park Adventure Playground, 1979.

Ken McCormick

We had our hearts in our mouths but luckily, the tyres hit a rise and flew just inches over the roof of the car! The driver was totally unaware of his lucky escape and we all let out a big sigh of relief.

We built structures from wood donated by local firms including the Metro, Vickers and Tyneside Timber. One day we had a call from Vickers to say there was some wood at the old Elswick Yard, which was being closed down. Some of it had been templates for tanks. We assembled them at the playground and the younger children had hours of fun playing on them. Unfortunately it was getting close to Bonfire Night, but they did make a great blaze!

Tyneside Street Press

Protests at Newcastle Civic Centre, October 1977, against cuts in adventure playground provision by the Recreation Dept who needed to save £40,000.

We set up an aerial runway across the dene to the west of the park. It ran from halfway up a tree diagonally across the dene to the base of another tree where there was a safe stop. It was about 25 feet off the ground in the middle. It was very successful until one of the older lads who was very big, wanted a shot. As soon as he started off, the rope began to stretch and sag. He was halfway down the runway when he went into some bushes and got stuck when he was still about ten feet high. He was not hurt, but his pride certainly was!

One of the good things about the adventure playground was the daily fire in an area away from the structures. We built seats around the area. As the children learned how to make fires they learned to respect fire; we had no accidents. In the winter, we had got some tea chests from Ringtons. When you took the inside foil off the chest, you always had some left over tea. We boiled water and made cups of tea for everyone to keep out the cold.

Ken McCormick

Hoppings time

I remember visiting the Hoppings wearing hideous brown and yellow chequered flares, plodging through the mud in my wellies, carrying my new goldfish. That was the year I won two goldfish – 'Charlie' from the Hoppings and 'Jaws' from a church fete. Neither of the fish lived for more than a few weeks. I came home from school to hear the bad news that Charlie had gone to the great fishy heaven in the toilet, but my parents had bought me a new Sindy caravan to make up for it.

I can also recall sausage and chips in the café on the top floor of the Co-op, sitting at the plastic tables surrounded by the smell of salt and vinegar and deep fat fryers, eating from a sturdy white plate and watching the people rush around outside.

Kirsty Ferry

The Hoppings, June 1975.

The Newbiggin Hall-E-Quins

I really wanted to be in our local Jazz Band, the Newbiggin Hall-E-Quins (like Harlequins, only Hall).

The Hall-E-Quins had around a hundred members so it was one of the biggest jazz bands around. There were only ten in the Blucher band. Members ranged from little tots of two or three right up to the Majorettes who were sixteen or eighteen. There were some lads who played the drums, but most members were girls.

There were lots of bands from different areas of Newcastle and Gateshead who would come to the Gala Field for competitions. There were around ten bands just in our area. There was quite a complicated league that depended on how the bands scored in competitions.

It seemed to be mostly men who ran the practice sessions. We had to go two or three times a week to the field; in the winter we'd be in Cheviot Middle School. I think they forgot we were kids sometimes, barking out orders. The routines could be quite complicated, criss-crossing and weaving in and out. The Majorette, swirling her mace, would go at the front of the parade with a little one behind her with a little mace, then the second Majorette and so on. It was a real family thing with sisters taking part. I didn't want to be a Majorette, the maces were so heavy, but I had a home-made one which was a broomstick with a decorated Squezy bottle on the top. I got a real mace one Christmas. It was metal with a big crown at the top and I could hardly lift it.

Our Comrades Club was twinned with Hemel Hempstead

Scotswood jazzband presentation, April 1974.

so we went down there and put on a display at a big competition. We went all over; one year the whole band was in the Edinburgh Tattoo. We went on our own hired double-decker bus. The mams and brothers and sisters always came along too. My mum has good memories of watching the jazzband on parade. She admired our pride as we displayed in our immaculate pink and blue uniforms and our ability to work together

I left before I went to the High School so I must have been thirteen, in around 1978.

Joyce Bell

The Dentonians

I joined the Dentonians Jazz Band when I was ten in 1972. The Newbiggin Hall-E-Quins were our rivals. Our crimplene uniform was smart navy blue trousers with a red stripe, and a red jacket with gold buttons, navy lanyard, and a sash for the medals. And of course there was a navy furry hat, with a red plume, rammed tight on my head. A silver kazoo completed the outfit along with whitened sandshoes and white gloves. The shoes could get really stiff with all the whitener. I loved that uniform, I was so proud to be part of the band.

It kept us off the streets all right. There was training two nights a week in the community centre at old West Denton Hall, or in West Denton High School, and we were away marching every weekend. There were carnivals every Saturday where eight or nine bands competed, and we went away to championships.

The weekly subs were only around 20p and you got your uniform and kazoo provided. Our trainer, Mr Larner, had the bright idea of using sausage skins as the buzz paper. We were terrified of him.

When we won a carnival the bus stopped at the end of West Denton Way and we'd march home along the spine road playing our favourite tunes – *Give Me Oil In My Lamp*, *Amazing Grace* (we wore that one out), and *Lord of the Dance*. And we'd already played the National Anthem on the playing field.

Dawn Soulsby

The Newbiggin Hall-E-Quins in Hemel Hempstead, mid-1970s.

Having fun in Leazes Park, 21 August, 1979, at Wap De Do Day. We have no idea what this was but health and safety doesn't seem to have been an issue!

Eldon Square shopping centre, 1976, just after opening.

Quayside, Spring 1973.

Mawson Swan, Grey Street, 1975.

Old Eldon Square disappears, 1973.

Bob Arkle, aged fifteen, from Ashington, snapped Eldon Square's new car park from Percy Street in 1975 during a bike ride into Newcastle to buy transistors from a little TV repair shop near the Co-op.

The Jimmy Carter procession arrives at the Civic Centre, 6 May 1977.

The demonstration on St Mary's Place was for Prime Minister Jim Callaghan's benefit. Workers at C.A. Parsons were anxious that an order for turbo generators for the Drax B coal-fired power station should be awarded to their firm rather than to GEC. In July, with some controversy, it duly was.

Above, the Quayside Sunday Market, 1976.

Right, preparations in the Grainger Market, for the Queen's Silver Jubilee celebrations, June 1977.

Paul Donaghy

Left. Our school football team taken on the yard of Sacred Heart Primary school in Fenham in the mid-1970s. A fantastic all conquering team of 9,10 and 11 year olds in school colours. That's my grandad – Reginald Brown – at the back, our number one fan who attended every game.

Paul Donaghy

Below, Hodgkin Park adventure playground, 1979.

Ken McCormick

Joyce Bell

Left. Every band had its own colour scheme. My Hall-E-Quins uniform was a pink and blue tunic and flared trousers (with a stripe), white sandshoes, white gloves, and a fur hat on top, square-on. You had to be really smart.

Joyce Bell

Kids going Clackers!

Clackers were everywhere one early 1970s summer. Two balls, like small snooker balls, on the end of a string that was fastened to a small plastic handle. The idea was to flick the handle so the balls clacked together at the top and bottom of a circle. The streets were filled with the constant noise of clacking. Many kids ended up with swollen knuckles, wrists and bruised arms. Maybe because of the injuries they inflicted, Clackers died out as quickly as they came in.

Dale Toothill

Kerry Bossons

Kerry's best presents, Christmas, 1976.

Elspeth Rutter

Polly Rutter, Myrtle Grove, around 1972.

Alex Cameron

Alex wins! Street party, Cavendish Place, July 1978.

Our West Jesmond swimming lessons took place at Byker Swimming Baths ... and one of our trips for a lesson coincided with the official opening of the Wall. I was unaware of the event until, as we exited the baths, we walked straight into the throng of a walkabout by ... Prince Philip. Without so much as trying we found a place in his path and stood to watch him come past. To our surprise, he stopped and talked to all of us. Noticing our wet hair, he asked if we'd been swimming and then he pointed at my Newcastle United shirt and asked me, 'Do you follow Newcastle?' 'Yes', I said, amazed that he knew one football shirt from another. 'And do you go to St James Park to watch the games?' 'Yes. My Dad takes me and my brother.'

Simon Donald (extract from 'Him off the Viz', 2010)

Prince Philip at the Byker Wall, 8 August 1974. Simon Donald is in the NUFC top behind the post.

The newly completed Byker Wall towers over Raby Street around 1975.

Home sweet home

Above, new housing in Heaton, 1974.

In 1971 we moved from Raby Street in Byker, where we lived in a flat above Ball's the Butchers. It had a tiny kitchen (which housed a bath under the bench) and a toilet 'hidden' behind a curtain. We were off to a brand new three-storey house in Heaton, where we had a bathroom, central heating and two toilets.

Shawn Fairless

Above, this suburban Newcastle home of the early 1970s was fashionably furnished by Habitat. The striking wallpaper was typical.

Marco Polo, one of the first pizzerias, Dean Street, 1976 ... Mateus Rose, candle light, banana split.

The first pizzeria that I can remember was Capanella's on Shakespeare Street. I thought it was wonderful. They served pizzas (I had my first ever calzone there), pasta and meringue glace. It was very cheap too. After that lots of other pizzerias opened, including La Stalla by the fire station. There was a regular disco there.

Kath Cassidy

Chris Rutherford

Medieval banquets ... a never to be forgotten feature of 1970s dining out ... included pungent bibs, tankards, wenches, mead, and a lack of cutlery. Lumley Castle was a popular venue.

Chris Rutherford

On the town

The tradtional pub ...
Cafe Royal, Nelson Street, 1976.
Some of the regulars were pleased to
sit for a bottle of brown ale or two. It
was a wild place especially on match
days. The exquisite pub windows
were badly damaged during a fight.
They were taken out for repair with
the intention to restore them when
the pub was renovated, but they
never were.

Richard Flynn

The modern way ...
The Geordie Pride, 1976, part of a
new concrete development on the
Grainger Street-Neville Street site was
heralded as 'the region's only
walkabout pub'. It featured a 35-yard
Victorian street with seating areas
behind mock shop fronts. At first it did
well, with weekly takings of £17,000,
popular with students from nearby
Charles Trevelyan College. A less
ambitious pub, the Green Dolphin,
opened nearby.

Left, eight GPO
girls standing on
the benches and
having a good
time at the
Hofbrauhaus,
1972.

Yvonne Young

Shaun Fairless

Above, La Dolce Vita, 1970.

Below, Spanish night out, Whitley Bay, 1977.

The Airport Hotel, January 1974, the favourite
dress is from Bus Stop.

Shaun Fairless

Whole Lotta Love

Angela Evans

We were determined not be dependent on either set of parents to finance our wedding in summer 1971, so we had only ten guests. The ceremony took place in St Gabriel's, Heaton and we had a buffet reception (£17) at Dickens (Carrick's Restaurant in Grainger Street). *(Ann Caddel)*

Ann Caddel

Lynn Steele

I was married in 1974. The dress, from Fenwick's, was £35. My hat was £10 from a milliner in the Grainger Market. *(Angela Evans)*

Mik Richardson

I was best man at my brother's wedding, my long hair neatly trimmed for the occasion by Salon 66, beard, suit and of course the platform shoes. To mark the formality of the occasion these were slightly lower than my normal club attire (a four-inch heel and green and tan panels). *(Mik Richardson)*

We married in April 1973 at the Civic Centre and the wedding was very much a family affair. We all went back to my parents' house in Christie Terrace, Walker, where my mam had arranged for caterers to do a buffet in the living room. *(Lynn Steele)*

My wedding day,
Newcastle Civic
Centre, 1975.
(Pauline Jobe)

Martin and I married in 1977 at St Gabriel's Church, Heaton.
My dress was an Ellis gown from Fenwick's French Salon.
The photographer was Harrison's, very trendy and expensive,
specialising in 'brides in bottles'! (Shawn Fairless)

I knew as soon as I saw it that it was the dress
for me. I spotted the Ossie Clarke dress in
Fenwick's, bought it and had it shortened to fit
before I showed my mother. (Joan Milne)

Above, outside St Joseph's Church, Benwell, early 1970s.

Above right, summer wheels, mid-1970s.

Below right, winter wheels in Scotswood, 1 January 1975.

CURTAIN RAIL
FROM
19½p
PER FOOT

5 BIG FLOORS OF EVERYTHING

1 PR ½ WIDTH REGIS TAPE
EASY CARE MATERIAL
COMPLETE

£14·16

5 BIG FLOORS OF EVERYTHING

VENETIAN BLIND
WHITE
COLOURS AVAILABLE

£13·85

5 BIG FLOORS OF EVERYTHING

£25·95

5 BIG FLOORS OF EVERYTHING

COFFEE TABLE

Sound of the Suburbs

The Members, 1979

House and Home

DEMOLITION IN PROGRESS

Left, Byker Wall show flat (furnished by Parrish's), August 1972; above, Portland Road, Shieldfield, June 1974.

Re-building Byker

From 1969-1983 Ralph Erskine's architectural office was based in an old funeral parlour corner shop in the midst of the Byker redevelopment area. I worked there from 1972 onwards, straight out of architecture school. We designed the Wall and several phases of low-rise housing, almost 2,000 homes in total, before new council housing was effectively abolished in 1980.

We had an open-door policy so that residents could drop in for information or advice, quite a brave move when people's lives were being reshaped by clearance and rehousing. It says something for the success of the scheme that we were able to stay there for fourteen years! Our English and Swedish team developed a good rapport with the Byker residents. We became involved in all kinds of community activities, from formal meetings to helping with summer fairs and helping to build experimental playgrounds, long before the days of Health and Safety.

Byker was a pioneering community project and fairly unconventional in appearance, so it raised lots of interest from politicians, planners and architects internationally.

Visitors came from far and wide and were often invited into people's new homes by the proud occupiers. The new homes, both in the Wall and the low-rise houses were built to good space standards with district heating and 'all mod cons', quite a contrast to some of the old housing with damp walls, outside toilets and, in one case, gas lighting. The generously planted landscaped areas and gardens were a real contrast to the old Byker of hard surfaces and concrete yards, with little open space.

Tenants were allocated their new houses six months in advance of completion at evening meetings held in our office, twenty or so houses at a time. They could swap to be nearer to friends and had plenty of time to quiz the architects about the details of the houses being offered. The contact with so many residents undoubtedly helped give a sense of community and ownership.

Michael Drage

Byker Wall, March 1976.

The Byker Wall is up, the old streets are coming down, 1977.

What can you write about Byker
When half of it's pulled doon;
There's potholes and there's puddles
Like the craters on the moon.

There's kerbstones up like gravestones
And muddy paths everywhere,
The dirt from the demolition
Is floating in the air.

They're putting up those concrete blocks
In a matter of days and hours –
I only hope the space they'll save
They'll use for trees and flowers.

Perimeter houses in Byker and,
An urban motorway,
Let's welcome in tomorrow,
Forget our yesterday.

Byker's the best place on God's earth –
You cannot match the folk.
All we need's new houses
Free from soot and smoke.

(From the *Byker Phoenix* community
newspaper, issue 1 1976)

Above, Beresford Road, Byker, May 1975.
Below, Byker Wall, March 1976.

It was exciting watching the old flats being replaced by colourful new houses. Growing up in Byker during the 1950s and 1960s the only greenery we saw was in Byker Park. In the new Byker there were gardens and hundreds of shrubs and trees. From seeing the odd sparrow or pigeon the area seemed to be filled with birdsong over night.

Lynn Steele

Our Byker flat

The flat we moved into in 1973, after our wedding, was in Harbottle Street, Byker. At that time the redevelopment had barely started. Harbottle Street was at the bottom of Raby Street, which had every shop you could think of. The upstairs flat had three bedrooms two of which were uninhabitable. The only heating was the coal fire in the living room. There was a tiny scullery and outside toilet. There was no bathroom or hot water, only a cold water tap and an old stone sink. However it was our first home and we made it as comfortable as possible. Lisa, the first of our three children was born there, and by the time we moved to Heaton, twelve months later, the demolition was in full swing.

In 1976 we moved back to Byker into another rented flat at the top of Commercial Road, owned by my brother Stephen. By this time Lisa had been joined by brother Garry. This flat was a step up as it had a bathroom and hot water, but still no central heating. The houses around were all demolished and for a while there were only a few streets and Bolam Street School left.

Lynn Steele

Lost!

We used to live in Harbottle Street but while I was in the Navy from 1972 to 1976 my mam moved to Gordon House in the Byker Wall. When I came out of the Navy the old Byker had been demolished and I spent hours trying to find where I lived as nobody knew their way around the new Byker.

Mark Keenan

Above, 3 March, 1975. Councillor Theresa Russell shows Byker residents an exhibition of the new housing development at Parrish's store.

Left, Byker Mission Christmas party, 1974.

Above, the Byker Wall, June 1974.

Right, a show flat dining area photographed in August 1972.

Gill Street, Benwell, May 1971.

Winter chills

I lived in a very cheap flat in Benwell at first. Businesses were closing down and houses were being demolished. We lived in a Tyneside flat on Armstrong Road. I loved it, though it was freezing cold and there was mould in the bathroom. One girl stuffed newspapers in the cracks around her window to keep the cold out. We'd pick up wood from the demolished houses across the road to burn on our open fire. And of course there was no vacuum cleaner – electrical items cost a lot. We had a hearth brush!

Geraldine McClelland

There was no central heating in many council houses at the beginning of the 1970s. Ours was upgraded in the middle of the decade. Before that we had one electric fire to heat downstairs. Upstairs had no heating at all. In the winters we used electric blankets or hot water bottles to warm beds. We weren't too bad though – we knew families that had more than one kid to a bed. Many of the old terraced houses were being cleared. Large new private estates went up, many built by Barratts. Chapel House, west of the city was one new estate that extended into Chapel Park and continued to grow and grow. This was probably the first generation of working folks to have the chance of owning their homes.

Dale Toothill

My parents' house was really cold. The bathroom was heated by a big electric bulb that was supposed to give out heat and light. I was about eighteen before we got central heating. Nobody had a phone. My aunty was the first person we knew to have a phone installed and she had a party to celebrate. We all got very excited just picking up the phone and listening to the dialling tone.

Joan Pattison

The wash house

In 1970 we lived in a flat in Clara Street, Benwell. Managing the family wash was a problem – with two children and my husband, Ron, there was always plenty of laundry. Salvation came in the form of my mother's neighbour, Emily who preferred to do her washing at the wash house on Armstrong Road and suggested I give it a try. I did have misgivings when mam muttered about battles in the wash house between some of the 'ladies', but Emily's washing was the pride of the neighbourhood.

The admission charge entitled you to the use of a 'stand' comprising a huge sink, bench and wash boiler. There were several spin driers and a drying rack. The drying rack had rods on which to dry the clothes and the whole thing slid into the wall. It was very hot and the clothes dried quickly. Large industrial washing machines could also be hired for a small extra charge.

Suzy, the wash house attendant, kept everything running smoothly. Some of the customers would hog the spin driers but Suzy would ensure that everyone got a fair turn.

Some women did mountains of washing by hand in the sink, using a

Armstrong Road, Benwell, 1971.

small posser or rubbing board. Normal rubbing boards had a wooden frame and a ridged metal surface where the clothes were rubbed to keep them clean. Emily used the Rolls Royce of rubbing boards, which had a ridged glass surface.

While everything was drying there was time for a cup of tea in the café. Woe betide anyone that was still there when her washing was dry. Suzy would charge in bellowing 'your washing's finished and you're holding up the next person!' A couple of hours in the wash house was time well spent. The week's laundry was done for a couple of shillings.

Mabs Taylor

Jesmond ... living the dream

Jesmond was very popular with young professional couples, many of whom had been students in Newcastle in the 1960s. They bought the Victorian terraced houses relatively cheaply, and settled in among the established community. Art Nouveau posters and William Morris fabrics were fashionable and it was a passion for that style that made Victorian housing so attractive for some.

Suburban modernity and newness was rejected by these young Jesmondites. They embraced the character of their houses – creaking windows, leaky ceilings, draughts and all. A hippy outlook went with stripped pine floors, occasional pieces of Habitat furniture, junk shop finds and hand-me-downs. Miller's Auction Rooms sold cheap furniture to strip down. Other standard elements were paper lampshades, macramé wall hangings, cheese plants and pop posters. Walk down Manor House Road or Devonshire Place on a sunny summer evening in the mid-1970s and the gentle sounds of The Eagles or the Byrds would drift from open windows as well as occasional smells of illegal tobacco products.

Osborne Road was a residential street and the Lonsdale and Brandling pubs were the centre of the suburb's social life. Dinner parties (maybe a stew followed by a high calorie pudding), were all part of the Jesmond experience. There was a variety of food shops including Newman's Delicatessen, which sold exotic breads and other exciting foreign delicacies. Wine was on the menu but most people were into home brew of various kinds, an 'interesting' and cheaper alternative to the limited range of cheap wines available to buy.

Outings were usually cheap or free – Sunday walks in Jesmond Dene and visits to Pets Corner with buggies and babies. Those people who had cars often owned rather shabby VW Beetles, Citroens and the occasional Saab or Volvo. Anti-nuclear stickers were highly visible in the back windows of cars and front windows of houses around Manor House Road and Holly Avenue.

Jesmond motherhood was an intense experience. The first generation of women to go to university in large numbers took motherhood seriously. Earth mothers adopted the National Childbirth Trust and Laura Ashley fashion – Victorian in style, flowered cotton smocks. They complemented the William Morris curtains.

Their popularity also coincided with the increasing influence of feminism and a resistance to the high glamour of Charlie's Angels or Pan's People. You couldn't bake flapjacks in sequins and Jesmond motherhood required a lot of time in the kitchen making and baking healthy foods, they were ahead of the game in terms of healthy eating. Health food shops provided lentils and muesli and other natural products like dried fruit, which was the alternative to chocolate for many a Jesmond child. Young mums socialised at a growing number of Mother and Toddler Groups and shopped in Acorn Road.

Hilary Fawcett

St George's Terrace and Acorn Road, July 1971 on a background of mid-1970s Laura Ashley material from Sue Cameron's maternity smock. Remember Leathard's, and Laws Stores?

The shock of the North

In March 1976, when I was seven months pregnant, I moved from Exeter to Heaton, Newcastle. What a shock the North East was! I remember going to Fenwick's to buy terry towelling nappies, washing them then hanging them out to dry in the fresh air. I was so upset when I took them in as they were covered with soot (people were still burning coal then). I felt so down-hearted and wondered why I had come to this dirty city. However, it didn't take me long to experience the friendliness of the Geordie folk. After my baby was born I was walking down a street in Heaton and a lady stopped to look at my new baby. She pushed some silver coins into his hand. I felt so welcome.

I remember feeling very lonely at home as in the 1970s there was an expectation that you would give up work. This meant living on one income and I remember not even being able to afford to have a cup of coffee at a café if I went into Newcastle. However, living in Jesmond was a godsend to me. Playgroups and mother and toddler groups helped me get to know other young mums and these saved my sanity. Jesmond was like a village and everyone knew everyone else. Lots of terraced houses were being renovated by young couples as family homes and saved from being split up into flats. Many of the folk who lived in Jesmond originated from other towns and cities and because of this did not have a network of support. Baby-sitting circles were commonplace and I remember these being run on a points basis (you had to baby-sit to earn points and then you used the points you earned to get someone to babysit for your children).

Sue Cameron

Jesmond families celebrate the Queen's Jubilee. Shortridge Terrace, 7 June, 1977.

Mandala Wholefoods opened in 1975 on the corner of Devonshire Place and Manor House Road in Jesmond and stocked things you simply couldn't find in the supermarket. It was run as a co-operative and the wage bill for the six staff members totalled around £100 a week in 1980 when this photograph featured in an article in The Journal. They had just had a pay rise to £1.25 an hour. On a good Saturday they might take £300. Everyone took a turn at all the jobs, including the VAT returns. Mandala was a Jesmond institution.

Before Mandala opened we had to go down to the Tyneside Environmental Concern shop in Walker for our textured vegetable protein and other veggie products. I loved Mandala, the smell of spices, the packets of tiny hunza apricots from Afghanistan that really did taste good, pulses I'd never heard of.

Anna Flowers

New from old: getting hip in Sandyford

In the mid-1970s the City Council was keen to encourage people to regenerate older properties so in 1977 we bought a rundown terrace house in Chester Street in Sandyford for £2,500 and received a £6,000 grant to do it up. This was a great opportunity for graduates to get on the property ladder. The day we moved in, in our ice blue Morris Minor, we'd been there for an hour and there was a power cut (electricity workers were on strike).

Around us so many buildings were being demolished, it was easy to reclaim materials to restore the house and we even had original pub doors that had Sitting Room etched in the glass. Perfect ! Antique shops were everywhere so it was affordable to create what is now a vintage look. This was era of pine and cream, Habitat influences, mixed with found objects, enamel signs, 1930s china and old velvet curtains.

From this experience emerged our business, Faulkner's, manufacturers of bamboo and cane furniture, based originally on Dean Street and then the Quayside. We sold Liberty fabrics, wallpapers, cards and luxuries like cocktail glasses. We designed and made furniture for the home and supplied a shop in Covent Garden with our range. This quickly developed into an interior design service for hairdressers, bars and restaurants as well as individuals. We were contracted to fit out the first gay night club Casablanca in the Haymarket, and the café in the Tyneside Cinema in a Deco style.

There were many new businesses starting up at this time and big chains moving into the region, realising that Newcastle was no longer a backwater. We were hip 'n' trendy and could party even in our Stack Boots!

Vera Faulkner

Vera Faulkner and friend outside Faulkner's, Dean Street, 1978.

Stoddart Street, just a few hundred yards from Chester Street, Sandyford, 1974.

Below, one of Faulkner's trendy bamboo sofas.

Vera Faulkner

The Tubes on stage at the City Hall, November 1977.

Right, fans storm the City Hall box office for tickets for a T Rex concert, 20 May 1972. (ncjMedia)

Play that Funky Music

Wild Cherry, 1976

Hawkwind at the Mayfair

My first experience of The Mayfair was on July 5th 1975, and it was quite an eye-opener for a fifteen-year-old. I'd won a competition on a local radio show, and the prize was a ticket to see Hawkwind. My dad wasn't too happy that I was going to a nightclub, but seeing as it was a prize, he agreed to drive me there and pick me up later. He had no idea what went on at The Mayfair but was a regular himself at the upmarket La Dolce Vita, so he assumed I'd have to look smart. I arrived at the club dressed in what I'd been wearing at a recent wedding, much to the amusement of the long queue of Hawkwind's notoriously 'druggy' hippie fans outside.

The management weren't going to let me in as I clearly wasn't eighteen (I looked about twelve), but as

The Mayfair, Low Friar Street, 1975, a dreary doorway but the scene of many memorable nights out.

I'd won the ticket, they agreed on condition a bouncer stood next to me throughout the evening, to ensure I didn't drink any alcohol. My wedding outfit was almost identical to his uniform: we had matching black velvet jackets and trousers, with white shirts and bow ties; except I was barely five feet tall, to his six-feet four. The two of us walked side by side down a flight of stairs and across the foyer, where a wild-eyed hippie looked us up and down and said aloud, 'man, these mushrooms are good'. Then the bouncer opened the main doors into the club itself.

The music was deafening, which I'd expected. So it was that first blast of hot and moist air, bearing an overpowering stench of smoke, sweat, patchouli oil and the dead-dog reek of damp Afghan coats, which I remember most. Once we were through the doors and my eyes had adjusted to the gloom, I could see we were on a vast balcony that encircled the room, above a dark pit where most of the audience was gathered. My chaperone's job was to patrol this balcony, and he clearly adored his work. Overly relaxed punters who'd slumped in a corner were dragged swiftly through the club by the hair and thrown onto the street, while I trotted along beside him. We made this trip four times while bystanders laughed and pointed at me, which he didn't seem to appreciate.

Marshall D. Hall

Having grown taller, Marshall D. Hall fronts Hot Snax in the late 1970s. The band had a residency on Thursdays at the Cooperage.

Hawkwind had a toweringly tall and extravagantly bosomed female dancer called Stacia, who performed naked. The band came on at 11.30pm, but a lad on the balcony with a pair of binoculars informed me that Stacia didn't usually make an appearance until later in the show. She made her entrance at midnight, just as my bouncer was beating a path through the crowd, so that I could make my way upstairs to meet my dad at our pre-arranged collection time. Her performance was the only thing my fellow adolescent mates were interested in hearing about the next day, so as far as they were concerned my evening had been a huge disappointment.

But the Mayfair itself had stolen the show for me, and from the age of eighteen I went pretty much every Friday night for many a year.

Later I was in a band called Hot Snax. We had a residency every Thursday at the Cooperage in the late 1970s where we built up a big following and released a couple of singles – one was John Peel's Record of the Week.

Marshall D. Hall

Like Punk happened

I grew up in a Mod household with an older brother and sister so we listened to Motown and chart pop music. All self respecting skinheads listened to Ska and Rocksteady and Trojan was the label to get it on, especially the *Tighten Up* albums. Big hits in the youth clubs were Desmond Decker singing *Israelites*, Symarip's *Skinhead Moonstomp*, Dave and Ansell Collins *Double Barrel* and my favourite, *The Liquidator* by Harry J. Allstars.

Top of the Pops was like a religion in those days. At 7pm on a Thursday night the streets were like a ghost town as everyone ran off to watch TOTP. Glam became big, Gary Glitter, Bowie, T Rex, Sweet, Slade, plus lots of weird novelty pop stuff like Chicory Tip.

In the late 1970s a huge change seemed to happen to music overnight, the Punk Explosion! Great bands popped up every week. Exiting new singles and LPs to buy and concerts to see at the City Hall or Mayfair. Music was changed forever. The 1970s ended with punk being commercialised, New Romantics moved in and decent dance music was almost dead.

Dale Toothill

So there I was, sixteen years old, and happy to be a budding hippy wandering round Newcastle's hippy shops in flares and beads, going to see bands that had their roots in the 1960s and early 1970s and just starting to feel like I belonged. Then suddenly something came crashing into our lives that turned everything on its head, split our friends and eventually got rid of the flares. That, of course, was punk!

The punk scene started in London but news of it soon reached us in the North. Stories of bands like the Pistols and the Clash travelled faster than the music itself and we were excited to hear about this new phenomenon that was apparently shaking up the music scene. The first time I caught some music was in Virgin Records one Saturday afternoon when the staff put on a video of the Sex Pistols. The whole shop came to a complete standstill as everyone watched this band snarling and glaring from the screen.

I didn't get to see the Pistols until a reunion tour many years later and I never got to see the Clash. They had a thing about not playing to the rich elitist students at Universities so when they appeared in Newcastle they played at the Poly which was ironic because at that time getting into the Student Union there was far more difficult that it would have been to see them at the Uni or even at the Mayfair.

I did get to see the first Stranglers gig at the City Hall just after their first album *Rattus Norvegicus* came out. The lead singer Hugh Cornwall stopped playing his guitar during one of the songs and performed his throat masturbation trick. He stood with his guitar flailing at his side, threw his head back and started to rub his neck with his hands, slowly at first but then increasing speed until he eventually launched a huge glob of spit into the air.

It was probably this that made the City Council take notice and the second time we saw them at the City Hall there was a row of wooden folding chairs at the back of the hall where some representatives from the council had sat to watch the band to decide if this was the sort act they wanted performing at their prestigious venue – or at least that was how the story ran. Either way he didn't perform the same trick at the second show! A few months later we saw the Damned, again at the City Hall, but they weren't as good as the Stranglers.

The great thing about being away from the London scene was that you could go and see punk bands but still be a hippy – you didn't need to take sides – although not everyone felt like that! One of the oddest pairings of acts I ever saw was proof of that.

In October 1978 I saw Hawkwind (although they had changed

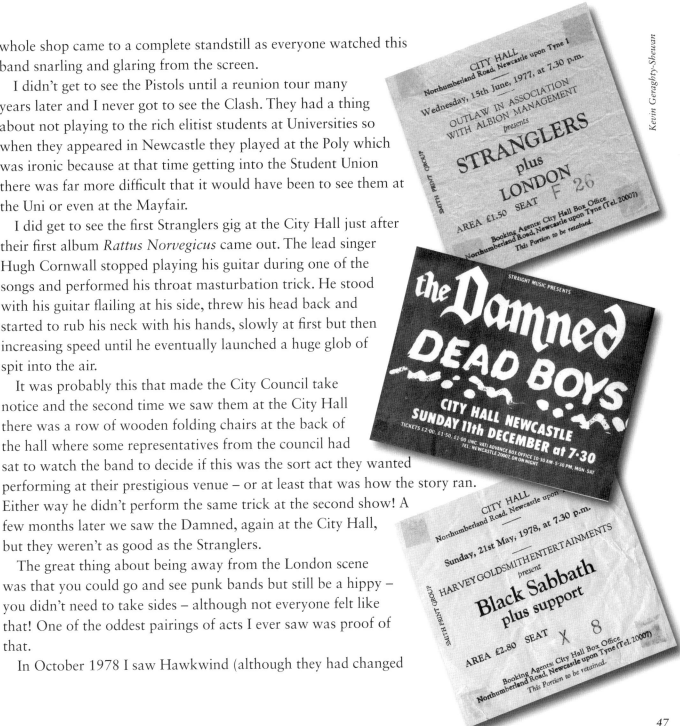

CITY HALL
Northumberland Road, Newcastle upon Tyne 1
Wednesday, 15th June, 1977, at 7.30 p.m.
OUTLAW IN ASSOCIATION WITH ALBION MANAGEMENT
presents
STRANGLERS
plus
LONDON
AREA £1.50 SEAT F 26
Booking Agents: City Hall Box Office
Northumberland Road, Newcastle upon Tyne (Tel. 20007)
This Portion to be retained
SMITH PRINT GROUP

STRAIGHT MUSIC PRESENTS
the Damned
DEAD BOYS
CITY HALL NEWCASTLE
SUNDAY 11th DECEMBER at 7·30
TICKETS £2.00, £1.50, £1.00 (INC. VAT) ADVANCE BOX OFFICE 10-30 AM- 5-30 PM, MON-SAT
TEL. NEWCASTLE 20007, OR ON NIGHT

CITY HALL
Northumberland Road, Newcastle upon
Sunday, 21st May, 1978, at 7.30 p.m.
HARVEY GOLDSMITH ENTERTAINMENTS
present
Black Sabbath
plus support
AREA £2.80 SEAT X 8
Booking Agents: City Hall Box Office
Northumberland Road, Newcastle upon Tyne (Tel. 20007)
This Portion to be retained
SMITH PRINT GROUP

their name to Hawklords at that point) and supporting them was a guy called Patrik Fitzgerald, the Punk Poet. He walked out in front of 2,500 Hawkwind fans armed only with an acoustic guitar and some short witty songs with titles like *The Bingo Crowd* and *Safety Pin Stuck in my Heart*. I thought he was absolutely brilliant but that was a minority view and eventually standing right at the front I still could barely hear him above the booing and jeering!

He stood his ground and finished his act despite the audience reaction and when he finished I knocked on the door at the side of the stage and asked if I could meet him. A few minutes later I was ushered into the support act dressing room, a cupboard compared with the one the headliners used. We chatted for a bit and laughed when we heard the Hawklords next door singing *Spirit of the Age* badly. After a while, and I can tell this story now my father has passed on, he handed me a joint and there, backstage at a Hawkwind concert I smoked dope for the first time!

Kevin celebrates getting a ticket for Led Zeppelin, 1979.

Kevin Geraghty-Shewan

My first encounter with Punk was when I bought the Damned single *New Rose* in 1976. I'd never heard anything like this thunderous wall of sound before, and that was it. My life changed forever. *New Rose* was quickly followed by the Sex Pistols' *Anarchy in the UK* and The Ramones' first album, then just about every punk single and album after that.

By 1975 music was getting stagnant and punk gave it the kick up the backside it needed. In 1977 the Sex Pistols released the single *God Save The Queen*. This changed everything; it was the Queen's Silver Jubilee and people's attitudes towards the punks became more hostile and violent. Suddenly we had to be a lot more careful – one minute people would cross the road to avoid us, and the next they wanted to punch us in the face. An appearance by the Pistols, drunk and swearing, on the Bill Grundy TV show didn't help.

In the early days seeing bands in the North East was a rarity, so me and my mates would hitch all over the country to see bands like Adam & the Ants, The Clash, The Cramps, The Rezillos (who I later roadied for) Generation X, The Damned and Siouxsie and the Banshees.

We slept in doorways, in the band's van or if we were lucky enough, they sneaked us into the hotel.

October 1978, Hawklords and Dr Feelgood advertise their City Hall gigs on a dismal hoarding beside the motorway. Above the Hawklords poster is the remnant of a Devo (American electronic band) poster. Dr Feelgood's Wilko Johnson (aka John Wilkinson) graduated from Newcastle University in 1970.

We didn't care how we got there or back. It was a carefree time and we didn't give a damn. Everything was a right laugh, even if it was at other people's expense.

As time went on loads of bands visited Newcastle and we could see The Buzzcocks, The Adverts, Wire, Electric Chairs and more at places like the City Hall, Mayfair, Poly and Uni.

By 1978 punk was becoming commercial, most bands signed to major labels and the music became more polished. Clothes were also changing: out went the rubbish tip DIY look and in came a smarter look, with winklepicker boots, leopard skin and animal print jeans, mohair jumpers, brothel creepers and almost no safety pins in sight.

Some amazing music was made in 1978/1979 by the likes of the Rezillos, Ramones, X-Ray Spex, Siouxsie and the Banshees and 999. For those few years we felt like nothing could touch us, we could wear what we liked, be as outrageous as we liked, and there was a real camaraderie amongst the punks at a time when we were treated as outcasts.

They were the best years of my life, but 1980 saw the end of punk. It mutated into something more violent and became a bandwagon for right wing skinheads. The punk look was dated and all the good bands were leaving the punk sound behind and changing into pop stars (although still making some cracking music). *Anarchy in the UK* didn't sound as inspiring in 1980 as it did in 1976.

Mitchell Whitehead

On Sundays we'd go to the Poly where there was a disco that mixed heavy rock with punk and new wave. Mohicans made everyone seem six inches taller than they really were!

Vanessa Histon

The Clash play Newcastle Poly Students Union, May 1977.

County Durham punk band Penetration, with lead singer Pauline Murray, right, were successful in the late 1970s, supporting the Stranglers at City Hall as their second gig.

Don't Take Away the Music: going to the City Hall

Getting tickets to see bands at the City Hall was a matter of making sure you got there before anyone else to ensure you got the very best tickets available. The first port of call was the recorded message that you could hear by phoning the Box Office telephone number. The message would list all of the shows on sale and inform you when booking would open for others.

In most cases the tickets would go on sale at 10am on Saturday, which would mean jumping on a train after finishing my paper round and heading over to Newcastle. We prayed that when we rounded the corner into Northumberland Road there wasn't a massive queue there already. Tickets occasionally went on sale during the week and it took a lot of sweet talking to get my mum to go and queue up for us, but she did!

Our first all-night queuing session was in 1978 for Eric Clapton. We arrived just after 6pm and though we were first in the queue we were soon joined by others. We spent most of the night talking to a bunch of students from the Polytechnic. This would prove to be advantageous when we needed someone to sign us into the Student Union for a Dire Straits gig.

A few months later we queued for tickets to see American band Rush. The difference this time was that it was snowing! It was very cold and our dad was dispatched to bring us home. However when he arrived he gave us some money for something to eat and went home on his own. When my Mum asked him why he hadn't brought us back he said 'Well there were too many people there to make them leave!'.

During the afternoon we had spotted a familiar face inside the City Hall. It was Den Hegarty, the former lead singer from Darts, who was doing some publicity for a new TV show that he was presenting for Tyne Tees called *Alright Now* (forerunner of *The Tube*). After a while he came out and we had our pictures taken with him. I've never seen them but apparently they were used, according to one of my school friends who was one of the 'Coffee Bar Kids' on the show.

It was a long cold night and we ended up in the Civic Centre car park at one point where some striking workers had left a brazier unattended and we huddled round it to keep warm. In the morning we were rewarded with tickets in about the fifth row (as the first few rows had been reserved for fan club members) but someone obviously told the band about us queuing in the snow because lead singer Geddy Lee mentioned it from the stage!

Kevin Geraghty-Shewan

Fans patiently wait on Northumberland Road to buy tickets for T Rex on 20 May 1972.

The first concert I was allowed to go to was T Rex in June 1972. I was 14. My friend's dad knew someone in the City Hall box office so we got fantastic seats, five rows from the front, in the middle. Marc chucked his towel off the stage at the end and it fell into my lap, but someone in the row behind grabbed it ... I was too slow! I also saw Queen as a support band (same seats) long before they were famous.

Angela Sutherland

CITY HALL
Northumberland Road, Newcastle upon Tyne 1

Monday, 3rd December, 1979, at 8.00 p.m.

HARVEY GOLDSMITH ENTERTAINMENTS

present

QUEEN
IN CONCERT

BALCONY £4.50   SEAT F 75

Booking Agents: City Hall Box Office
Northumberland Road, Newcastle upon Tyne (Tel. 20007)

This Portion to be retained

SMITH PRINT GROUP

Meeting Muddy at the stage door

One of the things about going to concerts at the City Hall was hanging around the stage door trying to meet the band or get autographs. You invariably attracted the displeasure of Colin Rowell, the stage manager, the road crew got pissed off with you being in the way as they tried to get all the equipment out of what was a very small door – but we still did it.

Some bands invited the fans into the dressing room a few at a time, others would come out and sign autographs in the street. The Tubes sat on their coach and we handed our programme or ticket to the tour manager who would pass them to the first band member and a few minutes later they appeared fully signed back at the door.

Meeting Phil Lynott of Thin Lizzy was memorable. He was still wearing the clothes he'd worn on stage, hair wet with sweat, a beautiful woman on each arm and a bottle of champagne jammed between his legs.

Sometimes the failures were more memorable than the successes. We had front row tickets for Eric Clapton. On the night of the concert I got to Newcastle early and was standing outside the stage door on the off chance of meeting old Slowhand himself. At one point a car pulled up but it clearly wasn't him. A few seconds later I became aware of an old black guy standing next to me while someone knocked on the door.

City Hall, 1971.

The guy looked at me and said 'Good Evening' and smiled. At that moment the stage door opened and there stood Colin Rowell who, with the words 'Hello Muddy', let the guy in. It was only when the door shut behind him that I realised I had been standing next to Blues legend Muddy Waters.

After the gig it was back to the stage door – there was no sign of Clapton. After a while the back gate opened and out came a man wearing a parka with the hood right up. Most of the fans were looking the other way but me and my mate Nick shouted 'Goodnight Eric' – the figure faltered in his step before walking quickly to a waiting car ... I'm sure we were right though!

When Black Sabbath played the City Hall in 1979 we were quite excited by the fact that a new American band by the name of Van Halen was supporting them. We had heard a lot of their new album on a local radio station and were looking forward to seeing them as well as Sabbath. While we waited outside a tour bus pulled up and to our amazement it was Van Halen. We all rushed over to the coach but as we did Dave Lee Roth got off the coach, held up his hand and said in an American drawl 'We're not Sabbath' and with that they walked off.

Kevin Geraghty-Shewan

The City Hall had a cosy atmosphere, with a seating capacity of approximately 2,000 (although not many actually remained seated). I even camped outside one bitterly cold night in February 1979 to make sure of a ticket to see Thin Lizzy. The ritual was usually the same - meet up with friends in the City Tavern, just along Northumberland Road. We had a drink or two in the City Hall bar before the show and then the anxious wait at the end of the gig at the stage door to see if there was a chance of meeting the band before 'legging it' in the hope of catching the last train home. I saw some of the biggest and most famous rock bands in history.

Simon Carey　　　*The City Tavern, Northumberland Road, 1971.*

The start of 1970 was an exciting time for rock fans in Newcastle. Led Zeppelin was to play at the City Hall for the second time within a year. I queued all through the night with hundreds of others, waiting for the tickets to go on sale in the morning. The atmosphere throughout the night was fantastic though rather cold! The concert itself was of course, brilliant. I had managed to get a balcony seat, although we were on our feet most of the time, and a friend who was in the stalls, took a photo of me in my tapestry jacket.

Christopher Baglee

Christopher Baglee on the City Hall balcony in his tapestry jacket, 1970.

In the early 1970s we went to what seemed like almost every concert at the City Hall. Tickets were about ten shillings, then about 50p or 60p. We saw all the big names of the time, including Wishbone Ash, Ten Years After, John Mayall, King Crimson, Led Zeppelin, Mott the Hoople, Genesis, Family, Jethro Tull, Lindisfarne, and our favourites, Free. At one of their concerts there was a power cut half way through so we all had to leave. They arranged another concert though so we didn't miss out.

Carol Rocke

The City Hall was a big thing for me. I went to see Hawkwind there and there was a naked woman on the stage dancing (she was called Stacia). My first wage packet was £8 a week but sometimes tickets were very cheap. I saw Jonathan Kelly with about three rows of other people, and Gallagher and Lyle several times. My friends went to see Cat Stevens and Genesis but I couldn't afford the tickets.

Joan Pattison

Probably the best concert I ever went to was Bruce Springsteen at the City Hall for the first time. He was brilliant. He had a real rapport with the crowd, telling stories and cracking jokes between songs.

Mik Richardson

Free played at the City Hall and were very poor – they appeared to be under the influence of some substance or other.

Albert Franchi

In 1972 a crowd of us went to see Bowie as Ziggy Stardust at Newcastle City Hall, with Bowie at his most outrageous and androgynous, posing like a femme fatale, sitting on the piano.

But the concert I remember the most was The Grateful Dead in 1972. We got to the concert really early and I got to chat to Pigpen (the harmonica player and organist), as they were setting up on the stage. The Grateful Dead claimed that this was one of their worst shows, with the most unresponsive audience of their career. We were all happy because we had seen our heroes!

By 1977 I was seeing Last Exit (Sting's Band) at the Gosforth Hotel. Gordon, as he was then known, had been engaged to my friend's girlfriend but they were still friends. I liked him a lot.

A few months later I picked up the *New Musical Express* and there he was on the cover as one of The Police.

Malcolm Henderson

Rik Walton

Jerry Garcia of the Grateful Dead outside the City Hall, 1972.

I saw David Bowie twice on the Ziggy Stardust and Aladdin Sane tours, Genesis (who were supporting Lindisfarne) and Lou Reed. His 'minders' came out into the audience asking 'got any coke for Lou?' and when he did appear he looked dreadful in a black leather suit covered with white powder. I also saw The Who at the Odeon. They smashed up the entire set at the end of the gig, but they were fantastic.

Kath Cassidy

An enthusiastic audience for the Bay City Rollers at the City Hall, 7 May 1975.

The Mayfair promoter

The year was 1970 and the date the 3rd of April and I had just concluded a deal to hire the Mayfair Ballroom every second Friday.

Rory Gallagher's Taste, with Black Sabbath supporting, was my very first venture and it proved to be a great night with Rory's guitar reverberating around the famous ballroom.

Later, I was to showcase The Who, Led Zeppelin, Derek & The Dominoes, Rod Stewart & The Faces, Deep Purple, Free, Chicken Shack, T Rex, Mott The Hoople, Quintessence and dozens of others including The James Gang featuring Joe Walsh who later went on to greater fame after joining the Eagles. My favourites included Rod Stewart, Deep Purple, Ten Years After and Free.

On 18th March 1971 I put the world's biggest group at the time, Led Zeppelin, on the stage. (The Beatles had split up and The Stones were in tax exile). I remember picking up Jimmy Page and Peter Grant at Newcastle Airport in my car and it seemed I had entered another world.

Robert Plant and Led Zeppelin at the Mayfair, March 1971.

I also recall Eric Clapton sitting in The Mayfair dressing room with his Strat in his hand as he played a few notes of *Layla*. He was quiet and unassuming and such a nice person. I realised promoting was not in any sense of the word a job, it was a pleasure, and one I still treasure.

There is of course The Who. Roger Daltrey failed to make it for the first gig as he had decided to drive up but became fog bound somewhere in Oxfordshire. With the other three members of the group already in the dressing room and 3,000 people in the ballroom, Pete Townsend and I had to go on stage to apologise and explain that the group would not be able play that night. Meanwhile, special guests Curved Air became the headliners and saved the day with an excellent performance. Fortunately, the crowd accepted it in good faith and all ticket holders came back seventeen days later and saw a magnificent show.

At Newcastle City Hall I promoted Captain Beefheart, Van Morrison, Led Zeppelin again, Free, Bad Company, Santana, Cat Stevens, Roxy Music, Procol Harum, Black Sabbath, Jethro Tull, and John Mclaughlin's Mahavishnu Orchestra. *(Find out more about Geoff's 1970s and his latest book, Three Minutes of Magic, at www.geoffdocherty.com)*

Geoff Docherty

Blondie to Beckett ... bands embracing the decade

Blondie: formed on January 1st 1970 by Tom Hill. Our agent, Ivan Birchall, had us working five nights a week by February. There were gigs everywhere, and audiences with insatiable appetites for the newer, the bigger, the louder, the heavier, the crazier and the sexier. Supergroups were coming and going faster than their groupies. We never stopped to catch our breath, or empty the ashtrays. Our constitutions were indestructible. They seemed to thrive on

Keith Fisher

Blondie, 1970. Keith Fisher far right.

abuse, and abuse them we certainly did. That year we played nearly 200 gigs between the Tweed and the Tees; our fees went from £12 to £65; we played The Mayfair, for example, ten times that year. If we had a run of days-off we drove to London and knocked on record company doors. In August, Kenny Mountain joined on vocals and Blondie became Yellow; but it was not until 1972 when Kenny joined Beckett – followed soon after by me and Bob in 1973 – that the London boys finally signed us up to a record deal – thanks in great part to our manager Geoff Docherty: the North-East's premier promoter. Tom, meanwhile, went off and formed Geordie with Brian Johnson of AC-DC fame, and they also found a bit of success so I'm told.

Keith Fisher

Blondie gigged from Tyne to Tees, but Beckett (above, 1974 line up by another brick wall) toured the country for a year; returning to the City Hall with Captain Beefheart; the Odeon with Wizzard; the Poly with Alex Harvey; and finally back to the City Hall with Slade. In between, a single and album were recorded, along with a performance on The Old Grey Whistle Test. Proclaimed by Melody Maker as one of two bands guaranteed success in 1974, Beckett dissolved later that year; the other band was Queen.

I was banned from wearing my Afghan coat in the car ... it took up far too much room!

AFGHAN COATS

Small supply flown direct from Kabul

Hand Embroidered in genuine Sheepskin. Various colours

NO TWO IDENTICAL COATS! EACH ONE INDIVIDUAL

ON SALE FROM 15th DECEMBER at:—

1st FLOOR, 36, ST. MARY'S PLACE,
NEWCASTLE UPON TYNE

EXPECTED PRICE £18 – £20

For advance information, telephone evenings Sunderland 71100

Having My Picture Taken

I photographed my first band at Rutherford College of Technology, which later became Newcastle Polytechnic, while I was an art student at Sunderland Art College. It was a double bill of Julie Driscoll and local blues band Downtown Faction (who later became Lindisfarne).

Through this I met Joe Robertson the Faction's manager. Joe had an office and shop in Handyside Arcade. He was an entrepreneur, constantly looking for new business opportunities, and decided that the coming thing was pop posters. He offered me £10 for every photograph that he used and gave me two tickets to the Rolling Stones in March 1971. When I got to the City Hall I discovered the tickets were for the back of the balcony! I made my way to the front of the gig and met the volunteer stewards who were very friendly and allowed me to take photographs at the front of the stage. From then on for the next fifteen years I just had to turn up at the door of the City Hall and I was allowed in.

Rik Walton

Mick and Keith, City Hall, 1971.

I think Joe only used three of my photographs but it was an entry into the world of music photography. I made no money from these early shots, I was primarily a music fan who saw it as an opportunity hear the music for free. However, it enabled me to compile a portfolio of images and to meet people who were able to offer me paid work.

My first real commission was to photograph the Newcastle Big Band led by the irrepressible Andy Hudson. They were playing the first Newcastle Jazz Festival and Andy used my photograph on their LP. The bass player was Gordon Sumner (AKA Sting) and this commission led to me photographing Last Exit who played regularly around the area.

For the rest of the decade I photographed bands both big and small at many venues in the region including the Cooperage, the Guildhall, Newcastle University and the Polytechnic.

Many of these bands are long forgotten like Deep Freeze, Whiteheat, The Squad (managed by Dick Godfrey, a local journalist and founder of Bedrock), Neon and The Edge (although their guitarist did join Oasis) but some like the Junco Partners, Archie Brown and the Young Bucks and the East Side Torpedoes are still going strong.

Punk was in the air at the end of the decade and the region's rising stars were Penetration who became, justly, one of the leading bands of the day. In the City Hall pogo dancing and gobbing became common and my friendly stewards often formed a protective cordon around me! The Boomtown Rats would pull a member of the audience on stage during the number *Having My Picture Taken* and to my horror I was chosen! For a moment I thought 'great opportunity for snaps' and then I just froze – I realised that my place was in front of the stage not on it!

Rik Walton

Neon at the Cooperage, 1977.

Newcastle Big Band

During 1974-5 I shared a flat with a friend of mine in Jesmond. We used to lead the bachelor life of late Saturday nights and lazy Sundays. We had usually recovered enough by Sunday lunchtime to wander down to the University Theatre bar (now Northern Stage) to listen to the Newcastle Big Band, a motley collection of about twenty-five musicians, led by Andy Hudson, playing music mainly from the 40s and 50s with a strong leaning towards jazz.

Newcastle Big Band, Andy Hudson third from the left, Sting fifth from the left, 1974. They are outside Andy Hudson's house in Jesmond.

In the rhythm section of the band were Sting on bass, John Hedley on guitar and Gerry Richardson on keyboards, who were three quarters of Last Exit, a band that we enjoyed every Wednesday, shoehorned into the upstairs room at the Gosforth Hotel on Gosforth High Street. We felt strongly that they had something really special and that turned out to be Sting. We were sorry when they stopped playing in Newcastle to try their luck in London, and I was very surprised and delighted years later when Sting popped up on TV with his new band The Police.

Although the Big Band was mainly instrumental Sting used to sing a few songs and their gigs always ended with him singing the Beatles' *Hey Jude* with the audience, by then several sheets to the wind, joining in on the long coda with arms waving in the air. It was always a come-down walking out into the daylight and fresh air afterwards.

One Sunday we arrived at the theatre to find the band set up in the car park watched over by a couple of policemen. Apparently a complaint had been made about the band contravening the Sunday Observance Act that barred the playing of secular music on the Sabbath. They were consequently banned from playing in the bar and in protest had decided to play outside. The usual crowd gathered around and the band managed to play a couple of tunes before the police brought the whole procedure to an end. They moved to the Guildhall down on the Quayside and for some reason they were able to play there on Sundays without breaking the law. Unfortunately the Guildhall lacked the tight packed atmosphere of the Theatre Bar and was brightly lit by the sun streaming in through the huge windows. It wasn't the same!

Geoff Laws

Newcastle Big Band playing in the University Theatre car park. Sting's head, with the full mullet, can be seen on the far left of the band. He had his amp plugged into the battery of his new 2CV beside him. In front of him is Andy Hudson the bandleader with his trademark nautical cap apparently chatting to guitarist John Hedley with the big afro. As you can see the band was heavy on saxes and 1970s haircuts.

A Brief History of Last Exit

I met Sting (or Gordon Sumner as he was then) in 1971 at Northern Counties School of Education, Benton. I was a keyboard player and in the year above him and had already formed a band. Because this band didn't have a PA, or a van, or an organ, the Student Union was our only venue because it had a piano and a PA. By the time Sting arrived in the first year, the student body was getting a bit sick of my Leon Russell impersonations. I discovered Sting was a bass player who had a drummer friend (Paul Elliott) who also owned a van, a PA and an organ. If I sacked my existing rhythm section we could go on the road ... So I did!

Despite my ruthless ambition that band hardly set the North East alight and the following year I found myself playing seven nights a week in a different band in a South Shields night club while Sting started playing bass with a cabaret trad band (the Phoenix Jazz Men) and the Newcastle Big Band.

Here he met John Hedley (guitar) and Ronnie Pearson (drums). John and Ronnie were older and more experienced than Sting and me but we all liked the same kind of music – The Crusaders, Tower of Power, The Mahavishnu Orchestra, Chick Corea, Herbie Hancock – broadly what at the time was called Jazz Rock. Sting was also quite keen on Folk Rock – Fairport Convention, James Taylor et al. We decided to form a band and with the help of Andy Hudson (Newcastle Big Band leader and also Newcastle Festival Director) managed to secure two weekly residences, one at the Gosforth Hotel on a Wednesday night, and, later, every third Sunday lunchtime in the University Theatre bar.

There was no great surprise on our part (as far as we were concerned we were going to 'the topper-most of the popper-most' – one of us was right!) when these residencies started to get packed out. We were 'Big in Newcastle!' This led to us supporting big name bands at the Poly and University (I remember Osibisa and Nucleus) and more work on shows at the University Theatre (*Rock Nativity* and *Hellfire* – what was it with

John, Gerry and Sting in the pit band for Rock Nativity, University Theatre, 1974.

Rik Walton

rock musicals and the Bible?)

Sometime in 1975 Terry Ellis replaced John Hedley on guitar and we got a publishing contract with Virgin. That contract also led to gigs down south and recording at Pathway studios in Islington. Both Sting and I were writing songs and tunes on a more or less weekly basis. This was mainly to keep the residency audiences and ourselves from going mad with boredom but there was a competitive element between us. Maybe I should have taken it more seriously. On nights off I would be in

Last Exit gig at the Imperial Hotel, Jesmond, 1973. Left to Right, John Hedley, Ronnie Pearson, Sting, Gerry Richardson.

the Cradlewell by eight o'clock knocking back pints whereas Sting would come down (after writing another bloody song) for a last drink at 10.15pm.

Last Exit was a very eclectic band. Funk, Blues, Folk, Reggae, Rock'n'Roll, Soul, Jazz Rock, Jazz Funk, Prog Rock, you name it, we played it. This was very good fun for us and the audience but really the kiss of death commercially. How would a record company go about marketing an unknown band that played songs as different as *We Work the Black Seam*, *I Burn for You*, *The Bed's Too Big Without You*, *Oh My God* and *Truth Hits Everybody*. All of these songs were in our repertoire but later reworked by Sting in a post-Police incarnation. One minute we sounded like Yes, the next Tower of Power, and the next Shakin' Stevens and the Sunsets. We thought we would be rewarded for our versatility not realising that record companies wanted bands with a defined image that was easy to market. Obviously after the gigantic success of the Police, Sting could and can be as eclectic and 'arty' as he likes but for an unknown band in the mid-1970s this eclecticism was a terrible idea. Then along came Punk to torpedo the already sinking ship!

While it lasted, Last Exit was an obsession and a vocation but being in the band (like any band I suppose) had its ups and downs. In 1974 (I think) we started playing a Sunday evening residency at the Newcastle Wine Bar on St Mary's Place. It seemed to be going quite well – the wine bar was kind of trendy and so were we (or so we thought) until about the sixth week when mid-evening and mid-song about twenty uniformed officers stomped into the place, told us to stop playing and started taking names, addresses and statements. Apparently we were breaking the 1780 Sunday Observance Law!

Somehow I became the fall guy for this heinous crime and subsequently appeared at Newcastle Magistrates' Court where I was convicted of 'Running a Disorderly House' and given a swingeing fine of £10. Andy Hudson (who was generally in the background with help and advice as an unofficial and unpaid manager) was outraged about this injustice and was interviewed on the local TV news with the Bishop of Hexham – an unlikely Last Exit fan! Andy then organised an appeal at the County Court and arranged for a barrister from London. The County Court appearance was a great success and this time the fine was quashed and I got an Absolute Discharge. The leading copper also got a right telling-off from the judge – 'I don't want to see any more cases like this in my court, Officer Bloggins'.

Of course the London barrister didn't come cheap so we organised a Sunday lunchtime benefit concert at the University Theatre to pay his bill. Predictably enough the police raided that as well but somehow we all managed to stay out of jail even though we kicked straight into the *Laughing Policeman* as they walked through the door.

Writing this has brought back a lot of memories – the time we got snowed in at Blakey Ridge, the night Sting spat on Alan Price's Rolls Royce, the A &R man from Island records who liked Dolly Parton. Readers who feel the need for more detail could do worse than have a look at *Broken Music* Sting's autobiography – most of it is true!

Unfortunately Ronnie Pearson died three of four years ago but the other members of the band are still around in 2011. John and Terry are both teaching guitar and gigging. I work at the Sage Gateshead teaching on the BMus in Jazz, Popular and Commercial music and run Gerry Richardson's Big Idea, a nine piece Hammond organ based band. We've played Manchester and Gateshead Jazz Festivals amongst other gigs in the last couple of years. Sting seems to be keeping quite busy as well.

Gerry Richardson

Lindisfarne's Geordie rock in the round: Newcastle City Hall 1976

By the summer of 1976 the original Lindisfarne line-up of Alan Hull, Ray Jackson, Rod Clements, Simon Cowe and me had been history for three years. Following the shock break-up of the original band in 1973 at the height of its success, we had all gone off to do other things. Rod, Simon and I had formed a new band, Jack the Lad. Alan and Ray Jackson also formed a new group, a different version of Lindisfarne with another four Geordie musicians.

Both of the new bands did well but it was easier for Jack the Lad; we started from scratch and created something new, touring extensively in the UK and Europe with great success, although the record sales were not as good as we would have liked.

The initial bad feeling created by the break-up didn't last very long. We were social animals and had the same circle of friends. By the summer of 1976, Jack the Lad had made three albums and were still touring but the Mark 2 Lindisfarne had folded.

Despite the fact that Alan, Jacka, Simon, Rod and I were now back on good terms, the original five members of Lindisfarne had not been in the same room for three years. It was around this time that an approach was made by the Director of the Newcastle Festival, that splendid chap Andy Hudson, to invite the original Lindisfarne to reform for a concert in a marquee on the Town Moor.

Before this, I had never considered the possibility of a

Rik Walton

Jack the Lad outside Newcastle Polytechnic around 1976.

reformation. I was happy playing with Jack the Lad and I knew that Alan Hull was concentrating on furthering his solo career and had no more intention of getting the band together again than standing for Parliament as a Tory. I had kept in close contact with Alan. I'd played on his first album, *Pipedream*, and had recently been in the studio with him to record his second solo venture, *Squire*. The album featured tunes used in Alan's first and only TV acting role in a play written by Geordie poet Tom Pickard. The others

Rik Walton

Harcourt's Heroes outside the New Tyne Theatre, Westgate Road, 1977.

were busy and equally disinclined to get involved. Ray Jackson had his own band, Harcourt's Heroes. What changed our minds?

At this point a young Geordie music business entrepreneur entered the scene. Meet Barry McKay who had owned and managed Oz Records while still a teenager. He was a huge Lindisfarne fan and also Ray Jackson's manager. He realised that the band still had a massive following that in many ways was more fanatical than ever – absence makes the heart grow fonder? He realised the potential of a reunion show and suggested we do it at Newcastle City Hall near Christmas time. Barry was right!

We got together in a rather down-at-heel Gateshead pub to talk things over but we'd only just ordered the pints when the empty bar began filling up and the autograph hunters started arriving. The enthusiastic reaction to the five of us being back on Tyneside gave me some indication of what was to come. As we left we agreed to give it a go.

Barry booked the City Hall for 23 December 1976. A second show was added on 22 December, and then a third at 6pm on the 23rd. Tickets all sold out in a matter of hours. BBC TV planned a documentary and a concert recording and Metro Radio signed up to record the show for broadcast on Christmas Day in competition with the Queen's Christmas Message. That's when we realised we couldn't back out.

We assembled at Alan's house in Whickham to rehearse in mid December. There was a cup of tea, a bit of small talk, the usual mickey taking but no sense of urgency. It was as if we were reluctant to actually start playing in case we sounded crap. Would the City Hall punters bottle us off and ask for their money back? Eventually we picked up the instruments and I counted in the first song on the list. There was a moment of silence and then we all fell about laughing. The ridiculousness of the situation had hit home, we were all scared to do the thing that we did best in case we were disappointed, but the music swung, the sweet and sour harmonies soared and we all had great big smiles on our faces. The magic was still there.

The shows themselves were a blur. We walked on stage to a fanfare on the City Hall organ, we had an ecstatic audience in front of us and our friends and family behind us on the choir stalls. When the band quit in 1973 there had been no farewell tour, no opportunity to say goodbye. Here we were doing it again and it seemed better than any of us remembered. It was a celebration, Geordie Rock in the Round. I swear every one of the 2,000 people in the hall joined in with every word. We seemed to have tapped in to a collective Tyneside consciousness that was unstoppable. We were their band, it was their music. At the end of

Ray Laidlaw

71

the show we left the stage but the audience had no intention of leaving. We changed out of our sweaty clothes but they were still stamping and cheering. This was a reunion show, a 'one-off', we were playing the old songs from the first three albums, we didn't have any new material. We had played everything we had rehearsed but realised that if we didn't go back onstage the audience just wouldn't leave the hall. Rather than go out and repeat something, we stumbled back on to the stage like rabbits caught in the headlights and Hully led us through an acapella version of White Christmas accompanied by the entire audience. Afterwards we had a 'knees-up' at a local hostelry. All our mates were there and we partied long into the night. I remember feeling a bit numb, I couldn't believe what I'd just lived through.

The reviews were ecstatic. 'How can you be objective about mass hysteria? All the misgivings were immediately removed when they took the stage; there was enough energy in the air to carry them through anything.' *NME* (a pretty positive comment from the music magazine that championed Punk and wanted to pension off all pre-1976 groups.)

The 1976 reunion was the kick-off for the second half of the Lindisfarne story, we got together again at Christmas 1977 for more shows and to record a live album *Magic In The Air*. We expected that the album would be a postscript and final farewell to the band. Again the reaction was ecstatic and the intervening twelve months had given us time to consider our options. We decided to reform permanently. In 1978 we released our first new material for five years. The single *Run For Home* was a huge hit and confirmed that we had made the right decision. We went on to make more albums, have more hits, tour the world with our unique brand of Country and Northern Music and return time and time again to Newcastle City Hall (over 120 shows in total). It got to a point where I became very possessive about the place. If a band played there that I didn't rate I felt a bit put out, like someone had been sick on my front room carpet. There isn't another venue like it anywhere, I know, I've played in them all. It makes me feel really good to know that the engine that fuelled Lindisfarne's creativity for another twenty-seven years was kick-started by the fantastic City Hall audience who welcomed us back to Newcastle on that cold December night in 1976.

Ray Laidlaw

Highlights of the year were undoubtedly the Lindisfarne Christmas Concerts, which became an institution. A party atmosphere was guaranteed.

Simon Carey

Lindisfarne Christmas Concert, 1976.

During the interval we made a quick dash to the bar as we were in need of a little refreshment. Thankfully I saw an empty couch and made a bee line for it. There I was, trying to keep seats for my family who were queuing at the bar, when a man slouched in and sat on the other side of the couch, I was a little peeved as it was obvious that I was trying to keep seats for other people ... a few minutes later the peace was shattered when a small army of girls came rushing in demanding autographs from the man. He was only Alan Hull!

Mabs Taylor

Sandgate

In February of 1971 a musician called Fred and I decided to form a band that rejoiced in the name Sandgate. Before too long we had recruited a full line-up and started playing at folk clubs (always willing to listen to original material) and working-men's clubs (not quite so broad-minded and a pretty tough audience). Many other local bands were

Charley Foskett, Paul Geleman, Keith Nichol, Jackie Ruddick, Fred Wheatley.

playing the same sort of venues; Lucas Tyson, Fogg, Brass Alley, Geordie and Beckett to name a few.

Within about a year I had left my job at a local printers and become a professional musician fronting Sandgate, and soon, having signed with a London agency, we began to play up and down the country at colleges and universities plus numerous gigs at the Mayfair.

MECCA OCTOBER 6TH. AT THE MAYFAIR NEWCASTLE ***
STEPPENWOLF
AND INTRODUCING THE JOHN KAY BAND WITH GUESTS Sandgate
8 P.M. – 1 A.M.
Tickets 90p in advance £1 at Door

At the Mayfair we supported bands such as Brinsley Schwartz, UFO, Steve Gibbons Band, The Electric Light Orchestra, the legendary Steppenwolf. We produced one single, which did pretty well locally, according to the Newcastle HMV record charts featured in the *Evening Chronicle*. We also developed our stage image quite a bit. I ended up wearing a sailor suit... don't ask!

By the middle of the decade Sandgate had disbanded and I ended up in another local band called Oasis ... yes, that's right... we had the name first! By the end of the seventies I had found my way back to the printing trade purely because of lack of money, but richer for the experience.

Paul Geleman

Junco Partners

The 1960s were good to the Juncos but we split up in 1971. We really didn't like hard work!

We re-formed in 1977 for the Newcastle Festival. I met Neil at a party and asked him to play sax and it all came together (as I said, we don't do anything hard). It was an ideal opportunity because it was the Newcastle Festival and our first gig was at Newcastle Playhouse or the University Theatre as it was called then. We didn't expect a big crowd, but when we turned up there were queues around the block, and the audience was very appreciative.

We went on to play most weeks at the Cooperage on the Quayside. And we're still playing ...

John Anderson

Junco Partners at the Cooperage, above, and, right, at the University Theatre bar, Neil Perry on sax.

All Around My Hat: The folk scene

Our club, 'Folksong and Ballad' was well established by 1970, in the Bridge Hotel, Castle Garth. Meetings were held weekly on Thursdays (residents and guest nights), and Tuesdays (ceilidhs and workshops). Our regular band, The High Level Ranters had established themselves among the major folk groups in Britain, with recordings, broadcasts, festivals and major concert performances. The folk revival movement was changing to include community dancing as well as song at venues around the North East.

One memorable event changed Tyneside – the publication by Frank Graham of *Larn Yersel Geordie,* (Scott Dobson). Suddenly large numbers of people became interested in having 'Geordie Neets' with songs, tunes, patter and imaginary working class Geordie clothing. Nineteenth-century local composers as Geordie Ridley, Joe Wilson, and Ned Corvan were elevated to a new status as creators of North East culture. A play was written about Wilson (*Joe Lives*) and performed to full capacity audiences, with a follow up documentary film on Tyne Tees TV.

The 'scene' had extended itself outside the folk clubs and ceilidhs to a more general public. Even the regional TV news featured spots in the vernacular! There was also a demand for Geordie singers in other parts of the country as the 'muse' enjoyed a new popularity.

Another development was increasing numbers of instrumental performers, meeting in pubs to play melodies from the repertoire of barn dance musicians of the past. Annual festivals were held, mostly at weekends, in Rothbury, Morpeth, Alnwick, Durham, Redcar and Newcastleton. Emphasis was on family-friendly events, with competitions for song,

Johnny Handle

Johnny Handle and the High Level Ranters outside the Bridge Hotel.

instrument playing and dialect poetry.

Towards the end of the decade, the young folk audiences of the 1960s had married and settled down, and numbers began to dwindle. While there had been a hundred or so each week, by 1980, figures of forty or fifty became common, resulting in fewer guest nights. However, many more people had taken up performing, so sing-a-round evenings were popular, and continued to be so.

Johnny Handle

Baltic folk

We had a brief flirtation with the Baltic folk club, down by the quayside in summer 1975. It was a small room, quite dark, with six or seven tables and a lot of people. Anyone could sing and I don't remember much instrumentation. I did sing just once, at my first visit to the Baltic – my one and only public performance – *Sprig of Thyme* with my husband, who treacherously dropped out after two verses. Unfortunately, after my first visit, I had to stay home as I was unwell, though my husband and friends went along on Friday nights without me. It was disappointing to find when I was able to go again that a bus curfew had cut numbers dramatically, so we never went back after that.

Steeleye Span played at the City Hall several times. Boys of the Lough were regular visitors to Newcastle. We went to see them in a fantastic concert at the Guildhall in September 1974 and again at The People's Theatre in October 1975. It was almost impossible to get drinks at the theatre bar during the interval, it was so packed, but we managed to slip across to the Corner House and back in time.

Ann Caddel

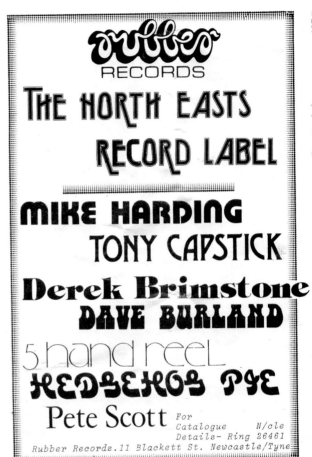

Ray Laidlaw (Lindisfarne programme, 1976)

rubber RECORDS

THE NORTH EASTS RECORD LABEL

MIKE HARDING
TONY CAPSTICK
Derek Brimstone
DAVE BURLAND
5 hand reel
HEDGEHOG PYE
Pete Scott For Catalogue N/cle Details- Ring 26461
Rubber Records.11 Blackett St. Newcastle/Tyne

Rubber Records label was established in Newcastle in 1971 with a sampler called Take off your Head and Listen featuring a variety of North East folk artists.

Hedgehog Pie

Rubber Records held a promotional concert for their first three LPs at the University Theatre in March 1972. It was reviewed in the local alternative newspaper *Muther Grumble*:

The last act, Tony Capstick – mainly a traditional folk singer – appeared traditionally bevvied and backed by Hedgehog Pie with a crate of beer. Tony Capstick has years of folk club experience, Hedgehog Pie have a great instrumented line-up. His voice, their whistle, acoustic bass, acoustic lead, violin and mandolin produced a well worked out sound. They immediately reached the audience with their brand of entertaining and skilful songs. They played a surprising range from 'Rambling Royal', lively instrumentals, to Dylan's 'To Ramona'. The act was almost cut short through running behind schedule ... although the organisers and anxious management still rushed around, Tony Capstick and Hedgehog Pie kept playing through orders to extinguish fags, take beer off the stage and finished the concert around two in the morning with all of them screaming 'Johnny B Goode'. The theatre was full.

Reproduced from *Muther Grumble.*

ncjMedia

Rubber Records artists, Hedgehog Pie, publicise themselves with a pile of pies in 1976 at Greggs in Gosforth.

Above, the Quayside was still run down and dreary in the 1970s as the Baltic Tavern, well-known for folk music, on Broad Chare bears witness. This photo was taken in 1968.

Above, right, Broad Chare, 1977. Nothing much had changed.

Right, serious folk on the Quayside, 1970.

The ever-popular Windows, Central Arcade, May 1979. Marcus Price women's shop was at the far end.

Hanging round the record shops

Apart from concerts the most obvious reason for going to Newcastle was to look round the shops, which of course meant record shops and hippy shops. In the Eldon Square Shopping Centre was the biggest of the record shops, Virgin. They had a huge range of records so if you couldn't get it elsewhere then this was the place to try. They also had a Now Playing board where they displayed the sleeve of the record playing.

It was at Virgin that I bought my first Gong album – *Flying Teapot*, which I got cheap because it had a small rip in the sleeve. They sold tickets for Led Zeppelin's Knebworth show in an early morning scrum during which my friend Debra's glasses got trodden on and she had an exam that afternoon. I also remember 'seeing' and hearing the Sex Pistols in there for the first time. They played a video on the TV screen and I remember being both excited and curiously disappointed at the same time. I bought their single *God Save the Queen* there in the week of the Queen's jubilee.

Windows in the Central Arcade was primarily a musical instrument shop and when we weren't drooling over the guitars in the window we would go downstairs where they had a record department but I don't actually remember buying anything in there. Across the road and round the corner was HMV. When Lindisfarne reformed they did a personal appearance there, signing copies of the new album *Back and Fourth*. The shop was packed to the rafters but in the chaos I managed to grab a copy of the sleeve off the wall display and get it signed.

Another record shop in Ridley Place was Listen Ear

Muther Grumble

The enterprising Richard Branson opened an early branch of Virgin Records on Ridley Place in 1973. Virgin Rags fashion shop was just up the road.

Virgin Records moved to the new Eldon Square shopping centre in 1977 and was replaced on Ridley Place by Listen Ear.

which specialised in less mainstream records and magazines. I bought my first copy of the *Fabulous Furry Freak Brothers* comic there and a copy of *Homegrown* magazine too. One night we went to see the Damned at the City Hall and with a few minutes to kill we wandered round to Listen Ear and were looking in the window when the police arrived. It turned out that someone had been seen tearing the tiles off the wall outside the shop and we were unlucky enough to be there when the cops turned up! Fortunately the police looked at our hands and clothes and decided that there was no way we could have been responsible and let us go.

On another occasion I bought Television's *Marquee Moon* album and had to borrow some money from my brother. It was only afterwards that we realised we didn't have enough money for our train ticket home so I had to pretend that I was under sixteen and pay half fare and even then we only had enough money to get to East Boldon (the stop before ours) – we were going to stay on but the ticket collector, whose suspicions were already raised, was looking at us so we had to get off and walk the rest of the way!

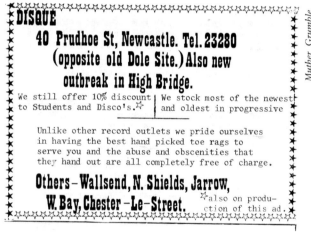

Disque moved from Prudhoe Street when the street was demolished in 1973.

No visit to Newcastle would be complete without a visit to Handyside Arcade. The only shop in there that sold records was the Kard Bar which had a few boxes of second-hand LPs. However our main destination was Fynd.

I used to love going there, it seemed to be a direct link back to the heady days of the 1960s when, we had heard, there used to be a club upstairs where Hendrix and the Animals had played. Local characters were always in attendance – I remember one in particular who was called Moondancer – who was always greeted with a strange reverence by us.

Kevin Geraghty-Shewan

The Land of Oz

Before I joined Hot Snax, me and my schoolfriends spent every Saturday afternoon in the early and mid-1970s hanging around Newcastle's record shops, which was a scene in itself. Oz Records, on Westgate Road, was a favourite, where we'd ask to listen to the most obscure and 'happening' bands we'd heard on John Peel, to try and impress the shop assistants. They had a set of aircraft seats where you could recline with headphones, and we whiled away many an afternoon there, smoking tabs and feeling impossibly hip. The old Virgin store on Ridley Place had a similar facility, but you always came home stinking of patchouli after a session in there.

Marshall D. Hall

Oz Records, which opened on Westgate Road in 1973, featured in Lindisfarne's 1976 Christmas reunion concert programme.

Ray Laidlaw (Lindisfarne programme, 1976)

HAPPY CHRISTMAS
FROM EVERYONE AT
OZ RECORDS.

RAY, ALAN and 'LINDISFARNE'S FINEST HOUR'.

You too can visit OZ RECORDS, enjoy a hot drink and listen to good music. You may not meet a super-star, but OZ RECORDS can offer you a nice atmosphere, hradphones, comfy coach seats, hot drinks, special offers, etc. OZ RECORDS stock a huge range of albums - everything from rock, progressive, pop, blues, folk and jazz to country, soul, imports, reggae, middle of the road, classical records and tapes. EVERY record and tape in stock at OZ RECORDS is PERMANENTLY REDUCED IN PRICE. Visit OZ RECORDS SOON!!

SPECIAL <u>LINDISFARNE</u> OFFER~

75p. off each of the following albums until January 1977. 'LINDISFARNE'S FINEST HOUR', 'FOG ON THE TYNE', 'DINGLEY DELI', 'ROLL ON RUBY' and 'HAPPY DAZE'.
ONLY FROM:- OZ RECORDS, 87 Westgate Road, Newcastle upon Tyne. Telephone (0632) 21812.

The refurbished Cooperage, 1975. It was lively all week long.

Right, Junco Partners at the Cooperage. *(John Anderson/Junco Partners)*

Ballroom Blitz

The Sweet, 1973

Get up and boogie

I could condense my memories into a night out. Aged seventeen, standing in a living room that was predominately decorated in beige and browns, peering through thick velvet curtains to see if my boyfriend was coming up the street. I'd be wearing my favourite loons, black and skin tight to the knee – then flaring right out in bright purple. Purple because I'd read in the *Jackie* that that was Donny Osmond's favourite colour. I was crazy about him. I'd have blue eye shadow and white 'shiner' on my eyelids and loads of mascara, despite my Dad saying 'Get that black stuff off your eyes!' Applying it could have been a bit of a problem anyway, what with all the power cuts. I'd be sitting applying my make up and then we'd be plunged into cold darkness for hours on end. It didn't affect my perm however. I do remember getting my hair tangled up in the bus conductor's ticket machine once. She just pulled it out, tutted and walked away.

Walking was a bit of a problem as my platform shoes were ridiculously high. Once I decided it was safe to cross the road, I would rock back and forth a few times, preparing for take-off, and have to thrust myself off the kerb! Political correctness was not a big thing then and my Dad used to say 'hey lass, you look as though you've got club feet!'

High Bridge, 1970. Opposite, The Oxford Galleries, 1971.

My boyfriend would have a droopy moustache, permed hair and a shirt with a huge collar, which would flap in the wind as we climbed into his Ford Capri and headed off to a restaurant to dine on Prawn Cocktail, Steak Diane and Black Forest Gateau. There were one or two pizzerias about and we might go to La Stalla for a change and boogie on down in the basement disco!

We went to see Lindisfarne at the City Hall where everyone sang along. We were out in time to go to the Man On The Moon for lager and lime then maybe down to the Old George to listen to more heavy music, mainly Led Zeppelin and Deep Purple blasting out of the jukebox into a haze of cannabis resin and cigarette smoke.

Iris McMenzie

We went into town shopping most Saturdays and had lunch in either Littlewoods café or Woolies café, which were opposite each other at the bottom of Northumberland Street. Most often we would have fish and chips or pie and chips. In the afternoon we went to the disco at The Oxford Galleries. You went up some red-carpeted stairs, checked your coat into the cloakroom, and immediately went to the powder room, all pink and beautifully lit. We thought it the height of glamour. There was a bar with the theme of a tropical island with palms and parrots. In the dance hall we would walk around in a line linking arms. Or we would go up on to the balcony to get a comfy velvet seat and check out the boys down below. We danced too of course. T Rex – *Ride a White Swan*, Norman Greenbaum – *Spirit in the Sky*, Mungo Gerry – *In the Summertime*, Jackson Five – *I Want You Back*.

Carol Rocke

Pub crawlers

Our main two drinking places were the Market Lane, commonly known as the Monkey Bar and the Chain Locker, downstairs in the Turks Head Hotel. The attraction in the Monkey Bar was the jukebox which was crammed with rock music, the most played track seemed to be *Voodoo Chile* by Jimi Hendrix. Having long hair at that time could be a bit dangerous as gangs of skinheads roamed the city centre with only one thing in mind – having 'aggro' with some hairies. Of course the odds were heavily stacked against the hairies and I remember having to bail out through the front entrance of the Turks Hotel as a gang of skinheads were waiting at the Chain Locker entrance.

Mik Richardson

As a resident of Gateshead, the first stop for me and my pals would be the first bar over the Tyne Bridge, the Market Lane on Pilgrim Street. It was nicknamed the Monkey Bar because a long-gone landlord owned a pet monkey that would run riot in the place!

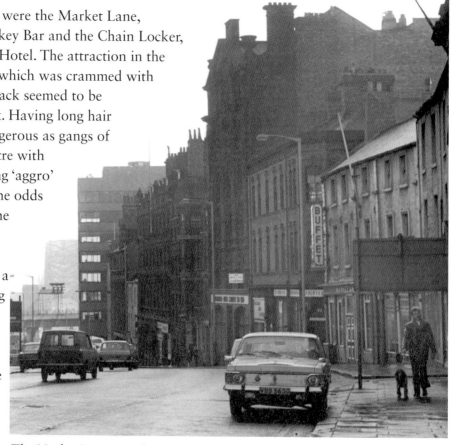

The Market Lane (Monkey Bar), Pilgrim Street, 1971.

After downing a few bottles of 'broon dog' we would move on to the Imperial in the Bigg Market. It was usually to the Old George after that, where the music ranged from Frank Sinatra to Deep Purple. The Rose and Crown opposite Farnon's was next on the list, followed by the Lowther and Carter's Wine Lodge. In around 1972 four songs seem to dominate the music in every pub, *Layla* by Derek and the Dominoes, *School's Out* by Alice Cooper,

Virginia Plain by Roxy Music, and *Hold Your Head Up* from Argent. The night inevitably ended up with a visit to the Mayfair, to throw up to bands such as Heads Hands and Feet, Vinegar Joe and Family. We saw in the dawn at Bower's restaurant nursing gigantic hangovers, before getting home to a rollicking from our mams at around 6am. Then at 7pm we did it all again! Ah the memories!

Peter Watson

Left, the Turks Head, 1968, and right the Old George, 1973.

Anyone could get served a warm lager in The Man in the Moon. You would navigate the stairs, no easy task with a maxi pinafore and clogs, and into the gloomy, smoky lounge – they couldn't tell if you were fourteen or forty.

Joan Pattison

You got off the bus at Worswick Street, started at the Adelphi or Bacchus, then to the Turk's Head and The Duke of Wellington (known as The Boot) then the Chancellor's Rest opposite the Mayfair and maybe the Lion and Lamb. There was much snogging and fumbling in the booths upstairs at the Mayfair if you were lucky. We drank Exhibition and Tartan beers that tasted like soapy water.

Albert Franchi

The Man in the Moon, Princess Square, March 1972.

The pubs were full of 'old' people – except for the Man in the Moon in Princess Square which was regularly full of underage people. Curiously, it changed its name to the Jubilee in honour of the national celebrations of 1977, although I recall it was one of the few pubs closed on the actual day, June 7th. (Roland Finch)

We'd start at the Man in The Moon, downstairs, dark and a bit of a dive. At a certain point in the evening everyone walked across town to the Old George. On the way we'd pass the Old George regulars who were on their way to the Man in the Moon. We all knew each other from the Mayfair, but never thought about drinking together on a Saturday. We'd stay at the George until shortly before closing time when we'd head back to the Man in the Moon for last orders. Of course, we'd pass the Old George bunch *en route*.

Vanessa Histon

High Bridge, and the Beehive Hotel, 1970.

All the Young Dudes

We'd go first off to the Hofbrauhaus on Waterloo Street where you could get a 'Stein', which was a litre of beer for the price of a pint. Oompah bands would provide the music and they held silly competitions like who's got the knobbliest knees, or who's go the weirdest underpants! It was a bit smelly from the kitchen at one end where they cooked burgers. There were big trestle tables that seated 40 people.

On the first floor of that building were Studios 1,2,3,4 and Scamps night club. That was on until 2am. We went two or three time a week so we knew everyone. It was disco music and twelve-inch mixes. I had a white safari suit, shoulder length hair, and a beard. I wore two-tone platforms, a big collared shirt, usually white, and a big silk kipper tie. I shopped at Marcus Price and John Collier.

As the 1970s went on my hair got shorter and I started going to Greys Club and La Dolce Vita where there was cabaret with people like Bob Monkhouse and Frank Ifield.

Stephen Patterson

The Dolce Vita and Mayfair were the clubs to be seen in until Scamps and Julies came along. Disco bloomed. Northern Soul flourished and kids went off to Wigan Casino or tried to make do with the Mayfair on a Sunday night. It was not quite the same.

As far as pubs went, the

Geordie Pride on Neville Street opened and closed and the Pineapple on Grainger Street packed them in. There was also the Monkey Bar, the Blackie Boy, and the Red Barrel by the Central Station. The Toon was always was jumping and I loved it! Rockers had their own bars in the Haymarket area. Pubs in the Bigg Market were mostly dives.

Dale Toothill

Haymarket, 1972.

Meet me on the corner of… (the Haymarket for example)' or 'see you at the Monument' were familiar phrases. With no mobile phones, a rendezvous had to be agreed upon well in advance.

My love of music, and in particular live music, led me to the Mayfair on Newgate Street on Friday nights and occasionally during the week when there was a good band playing there. At 2am on a Saturday morning there was no need to run for the train, there wasn't one! Unless there was a chance of a lift home from someone not drinking due to work commitments the next day it involved a long wait in the Central Station until the morning. Taxis did not even enter into the equation.

Simon Carey

The first place to visit was the Rose and Crown pub near the Swallow Hotel where the music was good and the people were there to be seen. Next stop was the Gay Trouper or Dive bar beneath the Swallow Hotel. The girls posed and finished make-up in the shop windows by the entrance.

The Dive bar had a juke box full of great music, Elton John, Roxy Music, Duran Duran, Bowie, Free all throbbed through your body with rhythms you could not resist. The girls were as decorative as the boys. White platform high heels seemed to be the shoes I remember most, apart from one girl who wore black thigh length boots and hot pants.

The abundance of colours in the bar was fantastic. Corners were occupied by kissing couples, (just out of sight of the management we hoped). Hot and sensual was the atmosphere in the bar and the music seemed to fill every particle of the night air.

The time came for the bar to close and we all trooped up to the Mayfair to watch the live band of the moment or to La Dolce Vita which had the edge on the Mayfair for class – the girls seemed better too.

John R. McCallum

The Pineapple, Grainger Street, 1970.

The first time I ever went for a drink in a pub was 1973 and I was only sixteen. My brother Nick and his friends took me to the Pineapple pub on Grainger Street. I remember walking down the steep stairs into what seemed to be a throbbing black hole. Argent was on the jukebox, and I was doing something illegal!

Shawn Fairless

Night Fever

In the spring of 1979 we moved from South Wales to Sunderland and when I saw Sunderland town centre I burst into tears. We lived in a bedsit in the middle of town and the first time we visited Newcastle at night was on a Friday evening, by bus. Several things were new to me: I'd never seen people go out with their 'party' clothes on without any coats, and the party seemed to start on the bus. Then we arrived in Newcastle and it was humming with hundreds more people in party clothes, milling around the streets and in and out of bars. What was on? There had to be something big we'd happened upon – a major concert maybe? We moved along with the crowds and navigated through the Bigg Market clusters and crowds, where it finally dawned on us that this was 'it' the destination was the streets and bars of Newcastle, an event in itself.

Annie Hodgkiss

Newcastle Life

Dancing on a cloud at Change Is, Bath Lane, June 1970.

Sophisticates

In 1969, in a layby near Penrith, my new Cortina was swapped for a rebuilt Vauxhall, hands were shaken and despite dire warnings we headed for Middlesbrough.

Two things kept me sane, Newcastle and Greys Club. Parking was a nightmare, but eventually we would arrive in Oscar's for drinks from the bouffant-haired barmaid, with perhaps a smoked eel sandwich. Then we were off again via Balmbras, Shakespeare, Duke of Wellington, Back Turks as fancy took us until around 10.45. Bill the doorman would quietly let is in, by-passing the pleading crowd in Greys Court, which once, to my delight included my brother, fuming in the cold as we ignored his request to sign him in.

The setup was fairly standard. The cabaret room with dance floor, bar and resident host, David MacBeth, singer Mirelle Grey and the Johnny Samson Trio. Downstairs, a disco guarded by Rasputin, the jovial bouncer. A restaurant playing continuous Barry White songs; a casino, sitting areas and the first video recorder we had seen showing the day's Newcastle and Sunderland matches. Both teams were regular attenders. In fact we drank champagne from the FA Cup the day Sunderland won it. Or could it have been a replica?

Actors filming *Get Carter* gambled there. Bernie Grant, the hairdresser, performed conjuring tricks, surrounded by a crowd of glamorous admirers. David MacBeth added to the tone of the place, likeable and humorous. 'Last Night at Greys' he would announce, twitching his glasses with a lascivious leer, as singers, comics, conjurers, ventriloquists, famous and infamous came on for Saturday night. Mirelle, his foil, sang *Dance in the Old Fashioned Way*, the band in the corner feigned boredom; champagne corks popped. The glamorous Wednesday gambling nights featured a superb buffet on a Swedish theme and the mystery silhouettes of the high rollers behind the silken hangings of the chemmy table.

Those were the days of hairdressers and expensive designer clothes, of adventurous cuisine and a feeling of sophistication and hope for the future. We had the best of it in the 1970s and undoubtedly I owe to Greys Club a large debt for preserving my sanity over a particularly stressful time.

Guy Hall

Greys

MR C. BAGLEE 'X'

Pumphrey's bistro and wine bar in the Cloth Market, around 1977. The Junco Partners are enjoying a drink in one of the old-fashioned booths. When Pumphrey's coffee rooms and shop were converted into a public bar after 1974 it was the start of the Bigg Market's transformation into a party venue. Pumphrey's went on supplying the trade from the Old George Yard.

Pumphrey's coffee shop had been the only place you could buy chocolate turtles! (Keith Fisher)

The Mayfair — Newcastle's finest
Ballroom and Banqueting Suite is
available for your Annual Dinner,
Dinner Dance, Private Function
for 500 - 2000 people.
Smaller parties from 10 - 500
catered for on specially arranged
evenings.

Contact us first,
at Newgate Street,
Newcastle upon Tyne,
Tel: 23109,
General Manager - Steven Lister.

*On Fridays we always went to the Mayfair,
a venue that was designed for cabaret and
chicken in a basket, but came alive to the
sounds of heavy rock.*

Vanessa Histon

**Every night's a Dinner Dance
with a difference, at Roys . . .**
Table d'hote or a la carte Tuesday through till Saturday 7 p.m.-2 a.m. Book a table or drop
in for the romantic candlelight mood.
Cabaret by Johnny Heenan. Swing to Ray Moores piano. Ron Studholme on the pops.

P.S. Beer at 20p a pint
Champagne up to £16 per bottle

ROY'S 2 ROOM Restaurant
Dining—Dancing—Cabaret
Licensed until 2 a.m.
VICTORIA HOUSE, GALLOWGATE, NEWCASTLE UPON TYNE. Tel. 24980

Eateries

In the 1970s I had a liking for Dry Martini and lemonade, which was widely advertised on TV, and Sobranie Cocktail cigarettes. These were long and thin and came in five bright pastel colours with gold foil filters, and were brilliant to co-ordinate with various coloured outfits. Boy, did I look cool with my Martini in one hand and my Sobranie in the other! During the day I would smoke More cigarettes, but they had to be the menthol ones because I felt they were healthier.

Every Sunday evening about twenty of us met in the car park of the Balloon pub in Fenham for a drink and then went on to follow either the John Miles Set or the Junco Partners. We followed them all over and I remember one time going to the Ashington Working Men's Club and being threatened with eviction because we were taking the micky out of the bingo players!

One of my favourite restaurants was Jim's Inn but we only used to go there on special occasions, mostly with my parents. They used to serve steaks on massive wooden boards and the condiments were served in little pots inserted into the boards themselves – delicious! If I wasn't having a steak then I would probably have Prawn Cocktail to start with followed by Duck à l'Orange.

Christine Dixon

Jim's Inn, North Street, 1972.

Wine and Dine at

Jim's

INN THE LEADING NEWCASTLE RESTAURANT

(Facing John Dobson Street)

Telephone 28741 for Reservations

Newcastle Life

For special occasions, such as someone's birthday, we'd go to the Eldon Grill where they served steak and chips and chicken in a basket. There was also a Chinese restaurant (the Sunrise) in what is now Waterstone's basement.

Kath Cassidy

One notable aspect of the 1970s – after a lifetime of dreary café food – was the appearance of the rapidly ubiquitous pizzeria, beginning for me in Shakespeare Street with Benny's La Capanella: hot and steamy, noisy but incredibly good fun, and a permanent party atmosphere from Italian waiters flirting outrageously with the tables of ravenous women; plus, the pizzas were excellent: buonissimo!

In 1973 a wonderful Yankee diner called Big Mamma's appeared on Low Friar Street, managed by Big Phil. It didn't last long unfortunately, so a little later, Stuart Young opened Dean's Diner on Dean Street. You could eat a genuine hamburger complete with sweetcorn or cucumber relish and a baked potato with sour cream. Baked potatoes were never seen in our restaurants until then. The poor offerings of McDonald's didn't even appear in London until 1977, so a 'beefburger' up here meant Wimpy.

Supernatural, next to the Central Library, opened in 1975 in response to Oodles – the London health food chain – and was extremely popular because you honestly felt you were not going to turn into a monster after eating lunch there every day of the week.

Next door, in what is now La Boca, was the Latin American Restaurant (the legacy remains in the signs on the toilet doors) who, apart from giving us our first taste of Mexican food, was also the first Newcastle outlet for American malt beers such as Schlitz and Pabst, Budweiser, and Colt.45 – served very cold; you could not get an extra cold beer in the North East until then!

Alongside the proliferation of Indian restaurants in the town centre there were countless Chinese restaurants dotted around because Chinatown didn't begin until the 1980s.

Keith Fisher

The Sunrise, Blackett Street, 1971.

When the RSC came to town I remember sitting in the Supernatural next to Judi Dench one year and Francesca Annis another, along the pine bench down one side of the room. They were really at the next table but it felt as if they were sitting next to us.

John Robson

The Milkmaid on New Bridge Street ... exotic Wensleydale and Pear Salad, iced coffee. At the Supernatural you risked losing your order of (rectangular) pizza, three salads, or goulash, as occasionally the counter staff vanished into the kitchen never to reappear. It was just soooo laid back, man.

Anna Flowers

A 'diet burger' at Dean's Diner was a hamburger with cottage cheese, a tinned peach half, and no bun!

Vanessa Histon

One of our first meals out was in Bimbi's fish restaurant underneath the Odeon. Martin ordered a peach melba, served in a slippery stainless steel cup. It landed in his lap.

Shawn Fairless

Florodor hamburger bar, Cross Street-Westgate Road, 1975.

Northumberland Street, 1973.
Right, a fashion shot from the Journal, mid-1970s. (ncjMedia)

You Wear it Well

Rod Stewart, 1972

Girls, girls, girls

There were two shops in Newcastle that no teenage girl in the 1970s could live without. I spent many happy hours browsing the rails in Bus Stop. I remember buying red hot pants with a big red flower on the bib, some very high-waisted trousers, cheesecloth tops and skirts, loon trousers and a brown blanket coat. My collection of platform and wedge shoes came from Sacha.

My best friend Gillian and I always shopped together and usually bought matching items. We wore them at the youth club disco at St Margaret's Church, Scotswood, where we danced to *Bohemian Rhapsody*, *Tiger Feet* and *Under the Moon of Love*.

Val Taylor

My first pay packet went on a fabulous Ossie Clark dress. I was mostly into vintage clothes and wore a lot of stuff from my aunt who had been a model in the 1940s. Bus Stop was my favourite boutique but I also bought quite a lot of clothes from C & A on Northumberland Street.

One must-have accessory was the long scarf as worn by Tom Baker, the fourth incarnation of Doctor Who. I crocheted myself quite a few in various shades of orange. These scarves must have been about 10ft long and one day mine got caught in the door of the No. 2 bus as I got off. Only the screams of a passenger saved me (but not from the telling-off I got from the driver) as the boa constrictor scarf tightened.

Shawn Fairless

Northumberland Street, around 1974.

Bus Stop (1972 above), in Northumberland Court, was an amazing boutique. The shop dazzled your eyes with clothes of poster paint colours, glamorous fabrics like satin and crêpe, shiny silver buttons and quirky jewellery. The boldest thing about it was the bright red façade – it beckoned you in to an Aladdin's cave of fashion. I only ever had one thing from Bus Stop, a bright red satin bomber jacket with big bell sleeves and a huge floppy collar. I loved it so much I wore it with everything, even my yellow, blue and purple mini-kilt.

Caroline Whitehead

I'd always loved fashion, so with my first pay packet I went to Bus Stop (where I'd never been able to afford to shop before) and bought a safari suit with a skirt. It was black with a design of palm trees and big pink flamingos. I also bought a pair of black flared trousers to go with it, then went to Sacha for a pair of platform clogs to finish off the outfit.

I always tried to buy something from Bus Stop with my wages. I had a brown crushed velvet jacket and skirt, and a panne velvet teal-coloured bomber jacket with huge sleeves. When my mother saw it she said 'You've paid £28 [a lot of money then] for a pair of sleeves.'

I also liked the Jeff Banks concession in Fenwick's, Victoria and Albert on Ridley Place, Boy meets Girl in the Bigg Market and Elle on Percy Street.

Kath Cassidy

My favourite shops were Sgt Peppers and Bus Stop for clothes and Sacha for footwear. My platforms had to be as high as I could get and the ones I wore the most were some black plastic boots that you pulled on and they stretched to accommodate your legs – looked good but boy did you sweat!

Christine Dixon

We wore loon pants, often by mail-order from *Sounds* magazine, or we made our own flares by sewing material into the bottom of jeans in a V-shape. We tie-dyed T-shirts and especially liked ones with long flared sleeves. We wore duffle coats with felt patches sewn onto the pockets. We loved to shop in Bus Stop. We thought it was so trendy and would visit every single Saturday to see what was new in. We all bought a version of a beautiful crêpe dress with batwing sleeves and a deep square neckline. Mine was brown with white spots. It also sold Biba make-up. The other shop we liked was the Clockhouse department in C & A. It was a little boutique on the top floor and it played pop music! At the time this was revolutionary.

Carol Rocke   *Fashion in the rain, Grey's Monument 1972.*

FASHION

Left, street fashion in Heaton, 1971.

Below, the Trend department in Bainbridge's, Market Street, before the move to Eldon Square, around 1975.

Public Image

Boy Meets Girl, Eldon Square, new logo and shop, sketch, January 1976.

The 1970s were a graphic designer's dream as there was a trend for redesigning logos and images throughout the retail sector. The buzz phrase at the time was 'corporate image', which meant designing a logo or brand and applying it throughout a company's stationery, signs, advertisements, price tickets, vehicles, uniforms and any other material relating to the business. Newcastle's shops showed an ever-changing face during the 1970s and just two examples of well-known businesses whose logos and corporate images were re-designed by Badge Group Design during this period were the Boy Meets Girl boutiques and Greggs of Gosforth.

Christopher Baglee

One cannot truthfully cover fashion without reference to the young and very 'with-it' element and we certainly found it at Boy Meets Girl in Newcastle's Bigg Market ... most outstanding to my mind was the 'wet look' dress by London Mob, midi-length with a tie-belt available in red and black. (*Newcastle Life,* September 1970.)

At Boy Meets Girl for autumn/winter big, bold, swash buckling look. Dick Turpin coats in lush, plush velvets nip the waist, flare out bravely and come in glorious colours ... peachy pink like sorbet ice or startling dramatic plum, or, for the over thirty who likes to be trendy but shies off the hot colours, there is a deep soothing black – looking very like moleskin. All at £16.95. (*Newcastle Life,* September 1971.)

COOL COOL CLOBBER FOR HE AND SHE

BOY MEETS GIRL

BIGG MARKET, NEWCASTLE
QUEEN STREET SHOPPING CENTRE
DARLINGTON,
AND SOON AT KING STREET, SOUTH SHIELDS

Get into GEAR HERE

NEW BRIDGE STREET, NEWCASTLE

city stylish

Also at ASHINGTON, CARLISLE, SUNDERLAND, HARTLEPOOL.

A fashion show at the nightclub Change Is on Bath Lane. Pictured centre is Jay Gould, managing director of City Stylish. These illustrations featured in Newcastle Life, March 1970.

The boys

Back in 1970 my waistline measured just under twenty-eight inches and the smallest fit men's jeans were often too loose for the demands of the day. Fortunately, the demand for broad belts with big chunky buckles persisted into the new decade and the best place to buy them was the Army & Navy store next to City Stylish; the youthful and accommodating chap behind the counter was Peter Harker.

Philip Harker and his two sons, John and Peter, had Army & Navy stores dotted around the town till 1971 when Plus Four appeared on Blackett Street and the start of a denim empire began.

Two years later they opened a second shop on Ridley Place, which was rapidly becoming something of a fashion Mecca. Another two years after that their third and forth shops opened on Grainger Street and Clayton Street; that's four shops full of denim and counting. When Eldon Square opened, the Blackett Street then Clayton Street shops moved into Sidgate and High Friars; although for one brief moment in 1977 they actually had five shops crammed to the ceiling with indigo in all its manifestations.

New Bridge Street, 1971.

The Harker brothers were not oblivious to the trading benefits of beautiful female assistants and had an arrangement with The Louise James fashion agency here in Newcastle to supply part-time and temporary staff to the shops on an ad hoc basis: so you may well have bought your Jesus jeans from the same girl wearing them in the advertisement. The photo shows a Lee promotion with models and staff outside the Sidgate shop.

Keith Fisher

Photo by Click Studios courtesy of Peter Harker

In 1973 I always wore suits, from Jackson's on Shields Road. I had a brown denim suit with loon pants and a fitted jacket, from somewhere like BHS.

Colin Boyd

My first suit came from Charles Blades in Whitley Bay. I was 16, so it was around 1975. It was a grey suit, which I wore with a maroon shirt and tie. At the time patent-leather two-tone shoes were popular and mine had slightly stacked heels and soles. They were blue and plum which went very well with the shirt and tie and the grey suit!

Later on Marcus Price was my favourite shop. I also bought clothes from Malcolm Macdonald's fashion shop in Newgate Shopping Centre. The cut of your trousers, flared or bell-bottom was all important. I remember buying a pair of Prince of Wales checked trousers with flares and turn-ups. They might have come from Isaac Walton's. I wore these with the maroon shirt, and a tank top.

My hair was short, quite trendy, not tragic, more mod than rocker, rather like Roger Moore as Simon Temple.

Anon

You had to be daring or you did not get noticed! I remember going out in white loon jeans, a white cheesecloth shirt with a purple velvet waistcoat with gold braid stitched onto it and the design was distinctly Asian. On my feet were platform ankle length boots in blue.

John R. McCallum

Alan Owen and Peter Watson, manager of Malcolm Macdonald, for the Exclusive Man. The shop, in Newgate Shopping Centre, opened in 1972.

go man
Shirts With Good Vibrations

Jackson the Tailor, Clayton Street, July 1976.

You Sexy Thing: the hair-do

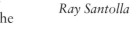

Ray Santolla

In 1970 Ray Santolla arrived from New York and started working at Luigi's on Northumberland Street, the nearest Newcastle got to a trendy, fashionable hair salon. He was almost immediately head-hunted by Paul Burton who was opening Browns in the recently built Newgate Shopping Center. This was really the beginning of the fashionable hair salon offering precision cuts in Newcastle.

Despite not being a hairdresser, Joe Robertson opened Wildes on Ridley Place in 1974 but brought Ray from Browns to manage it. Twelve months later Ray bought the place from Joe. In 1977 Ray opened the Cutting Garden in Eldon Square, giving the place a soft floral theme as opposed to the chrome and glass look he had in Wildes. At the end of his first triumphant decade Ray opened Sumi in the Big Market, decorating it in an oriental style. When I thought hairdressers in Newcastle I thought Ray Santolla.

Keith Fisher

Ray Santolla

I experimented with lots of different hair cuts in the 1970s, including the Purdey (inspired by Joanna Lumley in the *New Avengers*) pageboy, and the Farrah Fawcett Majors look that had flicks at the side.

Val Taylor

You could get a men's haircut at the Western Saloon at the corner of Worswick Street, or Henry's opposite the Central Station – decent barbers were few and far between. There was a back street barbers beside St James's Park that had packets of condoms in the window but I was too scared to go in and buy any! Something for the weekend, Sir?

Albert Franchi

My hair (cut for the Apprentice of the Year award, 1978) was courtesy of Bobby and Barry hairdressers around the corner from Newgate Street Co-op, not quite Brian Ferry but getting there. Bobby and Barry did a mean wedge.

Dale Toothill

Ray Santolla

CUTTING HAIR............AT 6 RIDLEY PLACE

MONDAY	—		
TUESDAY	10—6		
WEDNESDAY	10—6	Women's cut and blow dry	2·50
THURSDAY	10—7	Men's cut and blow dry	2·00
FRIDAY	10—7	Conditioning	·25p
SATURDAY	9—4	'Wilde's' set	1·25
		'Wilde's' blow dry	1·25
		Highlights	4·50
		Demi~wave	4·50
		Henna	5·00

All prices inclusive of VAT

MANAGER:
Raymond Santolla

TELEPHONE 25971 & 21752

Wildes, Ridley Place, around 1975.

Stylists sometimes insisted on cutting hair just the way they wanted to. My waist-length curly hair was cut in Wildes in 1976. The stairs were a bit tricky in platform shoes! I went in for a trim, and I came out with a bob which turned into a brillo pad once I'd washed and dried it myself.

After that I didn't go to any hairdressers for rather a long time ...

Shawn Fairless

115

The sophisticated lady, Enid Gowns

Newcastle Life

Between 1976 and 1982 I was proprietor of Enid Gowns at 11 St Mary's Place. The business was started in 1939 by Mrs Enid Marks at 3 Lovaine Row and in 1940 it moved to 18 Great North Road, next to the offices of the Automobile Association.

Mrs Marks and her daughter Elizabeth had a showroom for couture garments and ready to wear. They also had a successful make and design department specialising in wedding dresses, bridesmaids' dresses and evening dresses. Following the death of her mother, Miss Marks carried on the business until she was required to relocate as a result of the construction of the Newcastle motorway. Suitable premises were found at 11 St Mary's Place and the shop opened in 1973.

When Miss Marks decided to retire I bought the business. At that time I employed a manageress, accounts administrator, three showroom assistants, and five people in the make and design and alteration department. I was anxious to retain the traditions and high quality that customers expected from Enid, so I went to London twice a year for winter and summer buying. These visits involved viewing the collections, going to the international fashion fairs and most importantly placing my orders for future deliveries. Some of the fashion houses with whom I placed orders included Christian Dior, Benny Ong, Otto Graf, Feminette, Goldix, Jean Allen, and Benson Landes.

Dress and matching pants £17.95

I offered a personal service that involved visiting customers at home with a selection of clothes carefully chosen for that particular person. This was greatly appreciated by people who were unable to visit the shop. Generally the business was very active with a lot of loyal customers, one of whom was Dame Catherine Cookson.

Christine Luke

Enid Gowns, St Mary's Place, 1976.

Christine Luke

The story of Elle

I opened Elle Boutique with my husband Alan in 1966 so we were well established by the 1970s.

Our image was inspired by *Elle* magazine and we bought in clothes from other designers including Ossie Clark, Celia Birtwell, Lee Bender (before Bus Stop), Moya Bowler shoes (their designer June Mackereth had been at Newcastle Art College at the same time we were). We also bought designs from other fashion graduates, particularly Lizzie Tait Knitwear and later Lorry Marshall Knitwear. We ran these more expensive clothes alongside our own label styles.

Soon other stores wanted to stock Elle designs – local shops at first and later over a larger area of England and Scotland. We'd started up with a few outworkers but we had to change to using factories. At one point we were delivering at least two dozen of our famous velvet jackets to Bainbridge's every week, not to mention orders from other department stores and small independents. This long-line fitted velvet jacket with little ball buttons

Elspeth Rutter

Elle, Percy Street, around 1970 with 'hippy' windows. The zebra crossing outside the Hotspur was a danger to inebriated pub patrons! Below, Elle in the late 1970s, with dungarees and smart print cotton dresses in the window. The zebra crossing has been moved.

Elspeth Rutter

up the front was our biggest seller. Some customers had three or four in different colours. We also produced wide-leg linen trousers, needlecord minis and maxi skirts, voile blouses, waistcoats, jersey dresses, print dresses, moss crêpe everything – crêpe was THE fabric of the 1970s along with satin and crêpe de chine, anything that was feminine and flowed.

Our first customers from the 1960s were getting married and having children, like us (these two things still went together in the 1970s). So we made ranges of children's clothes, particularly indigo denim dungarees.

Ethnic clothes had started to appear in the 1960s exactly as worn in their home countries, Indian Kurta shirts, caftans from Morocco and Afghan coats. Very quickly the fashion business, which was now BIG business, realized that these traditional garments could be streamlined for the world markets and could be, 're-designed' for the 1970s 'free spirits'. The traditional

Druridge Bay, 1973. Elspeth is wearing a knit fabric tunic from Elle and platform boots from Biba.

blockprints, embroideries and fine work gave a big boost to the Indian economy and the Indian employers, and clothed the now massive youth market. Again we fitted these ethnic looks in with our own styles and our designer ranges. Everyone wore cheesecloth shirts, famous for becoming two sizes smaller when washed. (We stocked a slightly better quality of these). Once the quality of cheesecloth improved, we were making it into every style. We sold large quantities of velvet and cotton loon trousers, stone washed jeans (these usually arrived still damp) and fabulous Indian, coloured leather bags with side pockets, from small handbag size to weekend away size.

One of our customers was an older but elegant lady who looked fabulous in a brown velvet Ossie Clark dress with armhole slashes. She paid for this with a cheque, and Alan asked her to put her address on the back – no cards back then – 'of course' she said and wrote Elizabeth Duchess of Northumberland, Alnwick Castle. 'Will that be alright?' she said smiling!

In the late 1970s Paul McCartney parked his big Wings Tour mobile home outside the shop to ask the way to the University where they had a gig that night. Unfortunately Linda was busy in the van with the kids – she had a reputation for buying a lot of clothes – Stella and her sisters now say that they learned

Elspeth Rutter

The early 1970s at Elle.

Above

Left: Wide-legged linen mix trousers with wide waistband and side or centre zip. Worn with spotted cotton voile pussycat bow blouse.

Centre: Scottish designer Marion Donaldson's frill fronted dress.

Right: Elle cream linen mix coat with Cluny lace edging, very pale pink lipstick and lots of black eye makeup.

Right: Outside the Elle workshops on Leazes Park Road, 1971. The trendy Renault 16 had a matt black custom-paint bonnet.

Elspeth Rutter

about fashion by playing in their mother's walk-in wardrobes full of beautiful designer wear.

In the early 1970s two girls and two men with foreign accents bought some clothes from us. (We did sell some men's clothes, like Ossie Clark/Celia Birtwell print satin shirts, jeans and velvet loon pants and of course the famous shrinking cheesecloth shirts.) These four loved our clothes and asked if we would be interested in designing and making stage outfits for them. We assured them that we couldn't do private dressmaking – only manufacturing for the shop. They were disappointed but left, well pleased with their purchases. One girl was blond and one a redhead. Of course it was Abba, who were performing at the City Hall that night.

Penny Plain (famous for its encouragement and promotion of young hand knit designers), was also in the Haymarket area. They sold Anokhi, which grew into today's East. We all began as fashion graduates, and learned the business as we went along.

Elspeth Rutter

I bought this lovely navy velvet Elle mini-skirt in the early 1970s, when a size 12 waist measured just 24 inches. (Angela Evans)

In 1976 Elle celebrated its tenth anniversary in The Journal with a photo of Elspeth and her daughter Polly taken on the steps of the University Theatre. The dress was a popular style that ran in many fabrics. They were a favourite of cello and harp players because of the wide skirt. Polly is wearing a junior version.

Above, Geordie Cobbler, High Bridge, around 1973.

Below, the Eldon Square pencils, 1979.

Above, outside the Civic Centre, Spring, 1973.

Below community art in Harrison Place, Sandyford, 1977.

Henry Bannerman tank top, early 1970s.

The two-tone leather platform shoe, above, is early 1970s.

The boots, left, are from Sacha, Grainger Street, which sold sizes big enough for men to wear.

Levis boots, 1976.

Right, wedding guests, 1977. The Bonnie and Clyde look?

Below, a variety of suits and mullets, mid-1970s.

Below right, Malcolm Gerrie, co-presenter of Lyn's Look-In, TTTV 1976.

The boys

The mannequin above is wearing Wrangler cords, and John Wesley Harding shirt. Stephen Spencer wore them on nights out on the town, 1973-1976.

Inset, Boy Meets Girl, Bigg Market, 1974.

Right, the Co-op advertises in the Journal Wembley Special, 1974.

Seven ways to improve your scoring power.

Clothes like these really get results. They've a look and a feel that comes over. Good and strong. With these kind of looks you could be getting those kind of looks. You'll get into the way of it at the North Eastern Co-op.

1 Two piece suit in Polyester/Wool window pane design. Twenty two inch flared trousers with 2½ inch turn up. Two button jacket with sloping side pockets. Get it all together for **£35·00**

2 Bonroy Acrylic tank top in Navy/White or Brown/White. Tops at bottom prices. Just **£2·75**

3 Safari Style Jacket. Fawn/Linen type with Dark Brown suedette shoulder and pocket flaps and all round belt. Nylon lined. Good hunting at only **£13·95**

4 Casual jacket in Terylene/Cotton with knitted ribbed Nylon welt and cuffs. **£10·50**

5 Flared trousers with deep turn up, side pockets in line with side seam. Check them out—great value at **£7·25**

6 Black leather high tab casuals with P.V.C. platform unit sole. Sizes 6–10 including half sizes **£8·50** (Also in Brown)

7 Burgundy looks great! Try these for size. Light tan rub off style vamp panel. Sizes 6–10 including half sizes **£8·25**

Available at all major North Eastern Co-op Stores. Open a Personal Budget Account. Ask for details in store. Credit Cards Welcome. Barclaycard, Access and Provident at most major stores.

Plus Dividend Stamps- your big extra saving

PROVIDENT

Consumer Information Service
For information on the Society's facilities and services, please phone Gateshead 71542.

Save as you shop at the new North Eastern Co-op

CO OP North Eastern

The mannequins, right, are wearing garments from Lee Bender at Bus Stop. Left to right, Black and white Art Deco print 1973-8; pale brown plaid smock coat, early 1970s; brown argyle print suit, 1974.

The girls

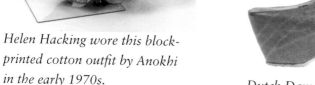

Helen Hacking wore this block-printed cotton outfit by Anokhi in the early 1970s.

Dutch Dames clog by Ravel, 1971.

In 1976 Susan Gardiner fell off this platform sandal. Luckily she only broke the strap and not her ankle.

Jean Varon dress, left

This was one of Mum's favourite dresses – she bought it from Fenwick's French Salon, when I was twelve, and I helped her to choose it. I can recall the huge changing room area with lots of mirrors and attentive staff. This dress was so unusual and elegant; Mum just fell in love with it – though she wouldn't have an occasion to wear until a ball at the Civic Centre three years later! It was by John Bates, one of the best British fashion designers of the 60s and 70s. Born in Ponteland, he went on to design for Diana Rigg as Mrs Peel in The Avengers, and sold his designs under the label Jean Varon.

Caroline Whitehead

Early 1970s mini-dress with matching shorts from Clobber at Fenwick.

All the images on these two pages reproduced courtesy of TWAM.

Clarks slingback, 1973.

Block print Indian cotton voile skirt with tiny 22 inch waist.

We sold lots of Lorry Marshall sweaters in this basic shape with slight differences in the detail.

Rainbow braces... these were worn a lot!

Ulla Heathcote knit tunic dress.

Lizzie Tait dress in wool, around £17.

Tuffin and Foale Liberty cotton lawn dress, bought in London.

We sold lots of these Indian leather bags at Elle, in a variety of sizes and colours. The smallest would sell for £3.50.

Biba shoe.

All photographs Elspeth Rutter

All the garments on these pages were sold or worn by Elspeth Rutter and family, who owned Elle Boutique on Percy Street.

Mr Freedom T-shirt.

Viscose print dress by Elle.

Left, plum acetate satin backed man's cowboy style shirt by Ossie Clark with buttoned bib front fastening and 'spaniel's ear' collar.

This blue velvet coat is by Ossie Clark, blue lily print by Celia Birtwell. It has deep pleats on the back and is very fitted on bodice and sleeves, in fact I couldn't bend my arms with it on! We probably bought just three of an expensive style like this and it sold for around £45. (Elspeth Rutter)

Right, block print shirt in crêpe, size 14, though it was a man's shirt. Sleeves were very full and gathered into narrow cuffs with the 'spaniel's ear' typical style Ossie Clark collar.

xix

BARRY McKAY ON BEHALF OF L.M.P. PRESENTS

Pallinson and Sons.–61 Blandford Street., Newcastle 1

LINDISFARNE CHRISTMAS CONCERT

FRIDAY, 21st DECEMBER, 1979, DOORS OPEN 7.00 p.m.

CITY HALL, NORTHUMBERLAND ROAD, NEWCASTLE 1

AREA £4.00 ROW R SEAT No 27

CITY HALL

Northumberland Road, Newcastle upon Tyne, 1

Thursday, 15th January, 1970 at 8 p.m.

Chrysalis present

LED ZEPPELIN

BALCONY 17'6 SEAT J 14

Phillipson Printers Ltd., Newcastle upon Tyne

Booking Agents: City Hall Box Office
Northumberland Road, Newcastle upon Tyne (Tel. 20007)

This Portion to be retained

GUEST

The Wildlife Action Group PRESENT

WHITEHEAT

PLUS

SHARPLICKS

&

AFTER-HOURS

AT THE PEOPLES THEATRE
Stephenson Rd. Heaton (NEXT TO CORNER HOUSE)

S&N BAR

6 p.m. – 11 p.m. Saturday 28th July

TICKETS £1 (£1·20 at door)
FROM WINDOWS, VIRGIN & LISTEN EAR

TICKETS ONLY AFTER 10 p.m.

Lindisfarne Back and Fourth

Geordie
Don't be fooled by the name

STRAIGHT MUSIC PRESENT

TED NUGENT

WITH GUESTS

STEVE GIBBONS BAND

CITY HALL~NEWCASTLE

SATURDAY 26th FEBRUARY at 7·30

TICKETS £2·50, £2·00, £1·50, (INC. VAT) ADVANCE BOX OFF. 10·30 a.m–5·30 p.m.
MON.–SAT. TEL. NEWCASTLE 20007, OR ON NIGHT

Simon Carey

Above, Simon Carey meets Mark Knopfler of Dire Straits backstage at the City Hall, 14 June 1979.

Far left, Geordie's Don't be Fooled by the Name LP appeared in 1974.

Police play the Mayfair, 1979.

Alan Hull of Lindisfarne, City Hall, 1979.

Blue Oyster Cult at the City Hall, 1979.

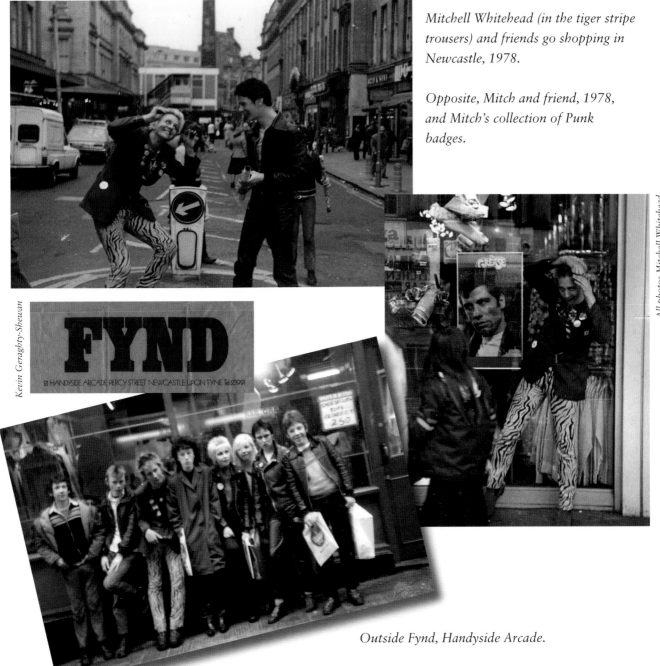

Mitchell Whitehead (in the tiger stripe trousers) and friends go shopping in Newcastle, 1978.

Opposite, Mitch and friend, 1978, and Mitch's collection of Punk badges.

Kevin Geraghty-Shewan

FYND

21 HANDYSIDE ARCADE PERCY STREET NEWCASTLE UPON TYNE Tel 23991

Outside Fynd, Handyside Arcade.

David Jobe

Days of Hope socialist bookshop had opened on the south side of Westgate Road by 1979. Politician Alan Milburn worked there for £20 a week at the start of his career and Mo Mowlam was a volunteer. Unfairly nicknamed 'Haze of Dope', the shop carried on the strong tradition of radicalism in Newcastle.

The European look: Marcus Price

Fashion in the 1970s became slightly more sophisticated. The 1970s were rough business-wise and the recession in the early 1970s stopped us in our tracks – we had traded for twenty years and done very, very good business and suddenly we were faced with not-so-wonderful business.

Fortunately we were able to pick and choose very carefully from a lot of imported merchandise. In the early 1970s we stocked New Man of France, which were classically French garments. We also did Marco Polo clothes which had a Scandinavian, European look. People had seen this sort of garment when they were away on holiday.

We also had a lot of three-piece suits made in Leeds, in various fabrics including tweeds as well as tweed suits designed by Nigel Cabourn. We were moving away from the American look.

By the end of the 1970s we were stocking much more expensive garments including Yves St Laurent. Not their top grade range, which was for their shops alone, but the blazer we stocked was £60 retail price whereas a Paul Smith two-piece suit would be £45. It was a very very big step up for us. YSL also did shirts and knitwear and that was the first proper

Tom, in the photo, was the younger brother of the manageress of Marcus Price in Blyth. We had eight shops during the 1970s, three in Newcastle. (Marcus Price)

Clothes from Marcus Price: Left, Marco Polo shirt modelled in the Bigg Market, 1975.
Centre, Hardware Clothing Co. pinafore, around 1975.
Right, fashion shoot for Julie's nightclub in Sunderland, mid-1970s.

designer wear that we handled successfully.

I remember that I got married in a fine black corduroy suit from Yves St Laurent, with a shirt and tie and creamy white shoes, which were pretty smart – I cut a dash! And I think Carolyn had a long suit, grey with large cream spots from Bus Stop.

I seem to recollect that everything I wore was black. When I was living on my own it made life very simple. I had a coat in quilted black velvet, a motorbike blouson in black with zips up the arms, and a satin blouson also in black.

Peter Golding was another designer who did some wonderful things and imported shirts from the far east. He made collarless black suits in wool crêpe. And they were marvellous. They made life simple again.

Marcus Price, interviewed by Caroline Whitehead

We opened the shop across the Arcade from us in Grey Street as a women's shop in 1973. We sold Marco Polo accessories and T-shirts, knitwear, blouses and trousers and silk skirts and tops. They were very beautiful things and they were different and very well priced. Hardware Clothing was based on sort of rougher type clothing including jeans but they became sophisticated too, in fabrics such as tweed and fine pastel cottons for summer. We did some absolutely marvellous frocks from Liberty prints. They were beautifully made and had a panel of another print in the bodice, say butterflies, it colour matched and was absolutely beautiful, they were very clever.

Marcus Price

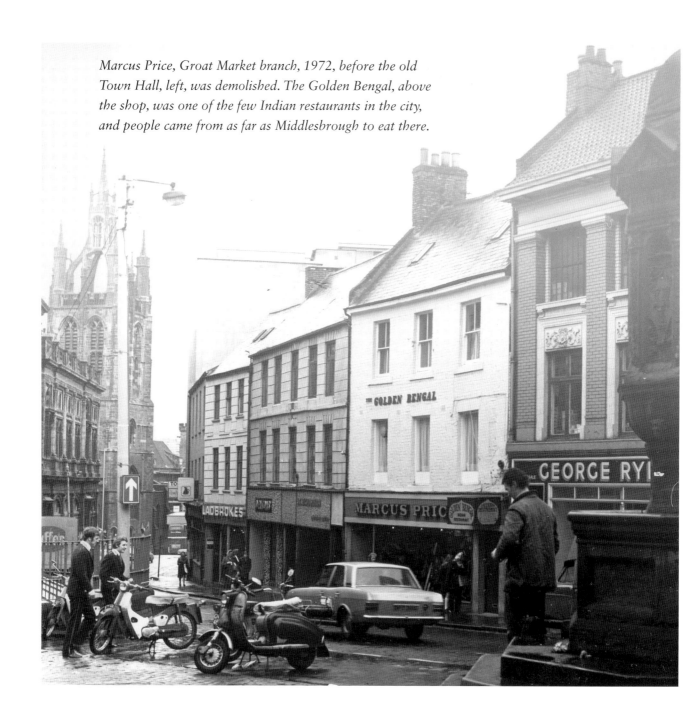

Marcus Price, Groat Market branch, 1972, before the old Town Hall, left, was demolished. The Golden Bengal, above the shop, was one of the few Indian restaurants in the city, and people came from as far as Middlesbrough to eat there.

The 1970s was a curious mixture fashionwise. At the cheaper end of the market trousers might have 32 inch bottoms ... that's as wide as the waist! And shirts were very tight. They just couldn't be tight enough under the arms and across the chest. The Grey Street branch was our more up-market branch. At end of the 1960s and beginning of the 1970s we'd sell ties in Percy Street or the Groat Market for ten shillings, but in Grey Street we'd sell silk ties for thirty shillings. We made a mistake by taking the Grey Street shop more down-market as the 1970s went on. The opening of the women's shop meant we doubled our expenditure.

Marcus Price

Hairies and hippies

I used to go round with my hair down to my shoulders, ripped t-shirt and ripped jeans and a pebble hanging round my neck. I imagined myself a true hippy. My parents were appalled but said nothing.

My mother told me some years later that one day she was getting on a double-decker bus and she spotted me sitting there in my finery. Shuddering she hid her face and went upstairs too embarrassed to be seen with me.

I knew I'd reached the end of the line when I decided to buy a multi-coloured string hippy bag, much in vogue at the time. I went home with the bag slung over my shoulder. Mam hit the roof. 'No son of mine is going around carrying that!!!!' The bag quietly disappeared.

Chris Mabbott

Lady Eleanor

In the mid 1970s I discovered Pre-Raphaelite painters and fell in love with the long flowing hair, the long flowing clothes and the sheer romanticism of it all. It was all very fashionable.

I washed my waist-length hair at night and plaited it while damp so that in the morning it rippled down my back. I wore long skirts (one was petrol blue crushed velvet) or pinafore dresses (ruffled at the hem and armholes) with cheesecloth shirts or smocks or granddad T-shirts with little buttons at the neck. I often wore a shawl. No make-up, just perfume, usually patchouli, musk or rose.

Elspeth Rutter of Elle boutique on Percy Street, models an exotic silk kimono for The Journal, May 1976.

My jeans were flared Wranglers. I hand-embroidered my favourite pair with stars. As soon as I left school I took the hood off my old grey duffle coat, shortened it and edged it with Norwegian braid. I sewed ribbons on blouses and embroidered them with tiny rosebuds. I made belts from scraps of leather and endless denim bags. I made myself a jacket from a remnant of cream brocade curtain material and hoped it would look regal and exotic but it always looked like an old pair of curtains.

My feet were rather less romantically clad in blue suede desert boots, red leather clogs or, in summer, Jesus sandals.

C & A was the place to buy clothes. I remember pink brushed denim flares with a silver rose embroidered on the back pocket and an acid green scoop-necked T-shirt with long flared sleeves printed with spotted platform shoes.

My favourite shop was Meander, on Mosley Street. They stocked beautiful velvet coats, dresses and jackets appliquéd

Penny Plain advertises expensive stock in Newcastle Life, mid-1970s.

with satin lilies that I really coveted. Unfortunately I couldn't afford anything that they sold. One of my friends had bought a jacket there and decided she didn't really like it, so offered to sell it to me for £5. I can still remember how happy I was. It looked like a Tudor fantasy in green velvet with red quilted velvet cuffs and a yoke in red, cream and green striped satin. I loved it passionately and wore it until it fell to pieces.

The boys I fancied had long hair (sometimes even longer than mine) and wore jeans (the more ripped and patched the better), cheesecloth shirts, granddad shirts, or a T-shirt printed with a band logo (Whitesnake and Yes were popular choices). They all wore denim jackets in the summer and the choice of an Afghan or an ex-army greatcoat in the winter. I tended to prefer the greatcoats as they were rather less pungent. Love beads were pretty much essential for both sexes.

Vanessa Histon

Above, street fashion outside Littlewood's, 1971.

Left and below, advertisements, 1974.

MEANDER is open 10 a.m. to 5.30 p.m. Monday to Saturday inclusive.

Fynd was the archetypal hippy shop with the overpowering aroma of patchouli oil and incense. It sold Afghans and kaftans and velvet shirts with flared sleeves (I bought one of those). There was always a beautiful hippy woman behind the counter and there was a candle shaped like a penis!

Kevin Geraghty-Shewan

FYND
JEANS
INCENSE
LEATHERS
JEWELLERY
N' THINGS
AT
21 HANDYSIDE ARCADE
Percy St. Newcastle
Tel. 22442

Courier

128

A completely different look

Skinheads were the big thing in the early 1970s. We wore high-masted (above the ankles) Levis and Wrangler jeans or cords or Levis Sta Press pants and Fred Perry shirts or Ben Sherman or Brutus dress shirts. Mint green Sta Press trousers worn with red socks were the height of fashion. The most important item was the Harrington Jacket. Steve McQueen wore them. The first Harringtons came in blue, black and maroon and maybe dark green and you had to have one. When my mother bought my first one, after weeks of asking, I hung it on the back of the bedroom door and could not sleep that night thinking about wearing it the following day.

Blackett Street, 1971. Burton's was a good shop for Mods.
In the colder months we wore crombie knock offs or parkas. Mobs of kids wearing crombies looked like a mass of mini Chicago gangsters. Some accessorised with pocket hankies and tie pins.

Dale Toothill

Doctor Marten boots, with the airwear heel tag and bouncing soles, were a must. My first pair was brown and I bought them from an older lad, second-hand and almost two sizes too big but I treasured those boots. I remember sitting on the front step polishing them religiously with bright red 'oxblood' polish, so deep it stained your hands or anything else you came in contact with. Later DMs came out with what we called 'astronauts' – boots that went up almost to your knees. The first time I wore them I was late for school because they took so much time to get into and fasten. We wore brogues and tassel loafers for school and some kids wore riding boots, with straps or without. We used to buy the riding boots at Marden Saddlery in Benwell – they did a roaring trade because of the Skins.

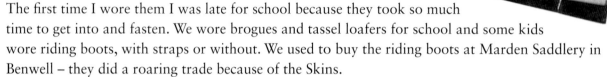

With brogues, loafers or riding boots it was fashionable to have steel tips in the heel and front. We bought segs and hammered them into the leather soles. Drawing pins were a cheap substitute and notice boards everywhere were stripped, especially at school. You made such a racket running through the school yards with the soles of your shoes covered in steel! They made shoes like skates, and kids fell or slipped, especially on stairs. Skins went to Henry's in Pink Lane for their cropped hair styles. Girls wore monkey boots, as did some of the smaller kids, and feathered hair styles, short on top.

Skins represented their areas, forming crews called 'agro boys': Big Lamp Agro Boys, Scotswood Road Agro Boys etc. Each area had a crew and fights often took place at the match or in town. We despised the kids with long hair that we called hippies or hairies. They hung out in the Handyside Arcade. The girls stank of patchouli and the boys were into heavy and prog rock. Skinheads eventually gave way to suede heads who wore their hair a little longer and dressed a little sharper.

Dale Toothill

There were four of us girls and our style was to wear Harrington jackets, with a zip and a woven collar, in black or red, with boots and tight jeans. I was the leader, and taller than the others and I wore bright red jeans from Bus Stop, the others wore black jeans with Doc Marten boots. I had rider boots, with elastic inserts and segs to make them click click click on the pavement. We were tomboys really.

Lorna Atkinson-Collins

Punks

All my mates got into punk and we made our clothes out of anything we could find. It was all about chaos, DIY and anything goes, the messier and more shocking the better.

I wore a bin liner shirt – just cut a hole in the bottom plus two holes in the side and there you go: one cheap shirt. We customized these with safety pins, chains and paint, and if they got damaged, we just made another one.

I got hold of a really tight pair of jeans, cut slits all over them and stitched in loads of zips. Pet shops were great places for studded collars, wristbands and chains.

T-shirts had their necks and arms cut out and slogans and bands names were written on with felt tip pen, in fact most clothes were destroyed and re-assembled DIY style, hair was made to look as messy as possible, and was spiked up with anything we could get our hands on including hairspray, soap and water, gel and even glue! Hair was coloured red, blue, green, etc with Krazy colour bought from the Kard Bar in the Handyside Arcade.

A few punks wore a swastika (myself included) but this was solely a shock tactic and there was nothing sinister in it at all. People, including my parents, thought we looked a mess, what an achievement!

As 1977 rolled on the DIY ethos got watered down by shops selling punk clothes, like Seditionaries and Boy in London. They sold Bondage trousers and jackets, all manner of controversial T-Shirts, like the famous 'Destroy' T-shirt with the swastika on it.

Mitchell Whitehead

Mitchell Whitehead

Mitchell, 1977.

Northumberland Street, 1971. The ultimate treat was to go to Fenwick's and have a 'Viennese Hot Chocolate' in the café. It had double cream on top with a Cadbury's flake stuck in it. (Patricia Fenton)

Opposite, the brand new Eldon Square complex, (glass replacing concrete as the material of choice) at the time the biggest in Britain, opened to shoppers in 1976.

Money, Money, Money

Abba, 1976

Eldon Square

My route home from school involved changing buses in the city centre, and I could not resist the temptation to visit the clothes department in Fenwick's or the cosmetics counter in Boots. The opening of Eldon Square was really exciting; it was fun being able to wander from Bainbridge's to Fenwick's without having to venture outside when the weather was cold. I loved using the covered walkway over Blackett Street and watching the traffic pass by below. For me at fifteen years old, Eldon Square seemed a magical world!

Grace Shaw

Grace Shaw (née Wong)

The new Eldon Square shopping centre had a huge effect on the whole retail experience. You could visit the numerous outlets without having to duck and dive shoppers laden with bags on narrow footways (especially during the festive period) on the cold, wet streets or dodge the cars and buses as they competed for territory. It was a warm haven, almost a sanctuary.

As I grew older I visited Newcastle on most weekends. Arriving at the Central Station, and depending upon which way the wind was blowing I was greeted by the familiar and seemingly ever-present smell of malt, barley and hops from the brewery. I visited all of the record and music shops and spent hours looking round the interesting side streets at the many second-hand/junk shops in pursuit of that elusive bargain. Handyside Arcade was not to be missed. It was a meeting place for a lot of people who would simply 'hang out' there, enjoying each other's company and generally passing the time. And there was always something mystical about the shops that sold an array of exotic clothing, materials and substances.

Simon Carey

Going into Newcastle was always a big event. In the early 1970s mam would treat me to a visit to Fenwick's and buy me lunch in Johann's coffee shop. However we'd only buy clothes at C & A as Fenwick's was just for window shopping. As a teenager I'd go to Newcastle with my friends and Handyside Arcade was our destination. This emporium of exotic taste was a mecca for us young hipsters, with its velvet jackets and embroidered cheesecloth, or dresses adorned with hundreds of tiny bells. We'd spend hours hanging out in shops such as Fynd and Bazaar looking at outlandish clothing and buying raspberry incense and patchouli perfume.

Claire Mason

Eldon Square opened to shoppers on 4 March 1976. It featured national stores such as Habitat and Mothercare. Tube downlighters provided illumination.

I was seven in 1977 and I remember the punks in Eldon Square. They would perch on the railing on Blackett Bridge, above Blackett Street. The walkway then was only a few feet wide with a metal railing down the centre. You walked on the left hand side going across and on the other side when returning, so it was a real bottleneck. The punks took advantage of this by leaning over and menacing people, especially us children. (B.A. Brown)

My older sister was bought the most outrageous shoes. Big platform heels with yellow, pink, green and purple leather clashing horribly together in a riot of colour that made her look like an extra from *Godspell*. I saw *Godpsell* and fell in love with the leading man and sang *Day by Day* for weeks afterwards.

Claire Mason

Saturdays on Percy Street

Saturday mornings in 1971 meant an early start for the weekly visit to the town. Being Hairies, the town was safer for my friends and me than estates with their gangs of marauding Skinheads. As men my age will confirm, we spent much of our youth running, not always for exercise.

We'd get off the bus in the Haymarket and walk along Percy Street to our first stop, Handyside Arcade, home to the Kard Bar, where we bought posters for our bedroom walls and patches for our denims. We only wore Levis or Wranglers, but people favoured one or the other. I was a Levi boy. On our feet we wore Bumper Boots.

After Kard Bar we'd go to Fynd, full of treasures from the East, candles and joss sticks and the almost overpowering smell of patchouli. It was a great place to gaze at willowy girls with long hair and even longer purple skirts, usually topped with a black velvet jacket.

Just along Percy Street was Jeavon's Music shop where you could listen to music in booths and gaze longingly at Gibson or Les Paul guitars, as played by all our heroes. Unfortunately, the guitars were almost as unattainable as the girls in the long purple skirts.

After Jeavon's we'd find a café, for a Coke and a sausage roll. Kids these days are spoilt for choice when it comes to places to eat or somewhere to while away an hour. In the 70s, I remember cafés were distinctly downmarket, like Chipvines on the corner of Shakespeare Street, opposite Pilgrim Street Fire Station. Like the adjacent Public Lavatories, the café is long gone.

Tony Metcalf

Sew on patch, ref. 50, 30p.

SMILE JESUS LOVES YOU
...n patch, ref. 4, 30p.

KARD BAR
POSTERS
ARCADIA · PRINTS
PERCY STREET · PATCHES
· CARDS
Tel. 28688

Some of us fancied ourselves as musicians, so Saturdays always included a tour of Newcastle's instrument shops. Millard's on Clayton Street and Jeavon's on Percy Street sold mainly entry-level equipment, for which we beginners were better suited, but Rock City definitely catered for the professional end of the market. Here you could ask to try an instrument with a view to buying it, and this was the place we'd choose to spend a couple of hours, demonstrating new chords that one of us had learned or invented, and checking how it sounded on a variety of expensive guitars through a hundred-watt amplifier at maximum volume. I can still remember the eyes of the staff glazing over, as

Percy Street, 1970. The south entrance to Handyside Arcade is beyond Faglemans, Jeavon's is further along.

they had to listen to yet another window-rattling attempt at the intro to *Smoke On The Water*. Maybe one us would buy a plectrum on the way out.

Marshall D. Hall

Lady Jane boutique next door to Philip Harker's Army and Navy Stores at the corner of Leazes Park Road, 1972.

Happy memories of Handyside Arcade ... eccentric and unusual shops like Fine Feathers (high class second hand clothes and a fantastic line in fur coats); Fynd (hippy clothing, smelly Afghan coats, joss sticks) run by the infamous Derek who then went on to open the equally infamous Barn restaurant at the top of the Arcade; and of course The Little Shop run by John Smith right at the back of the Arcade, where you could get really cheap second-hand furniture and antiques.

Lesley Oakden

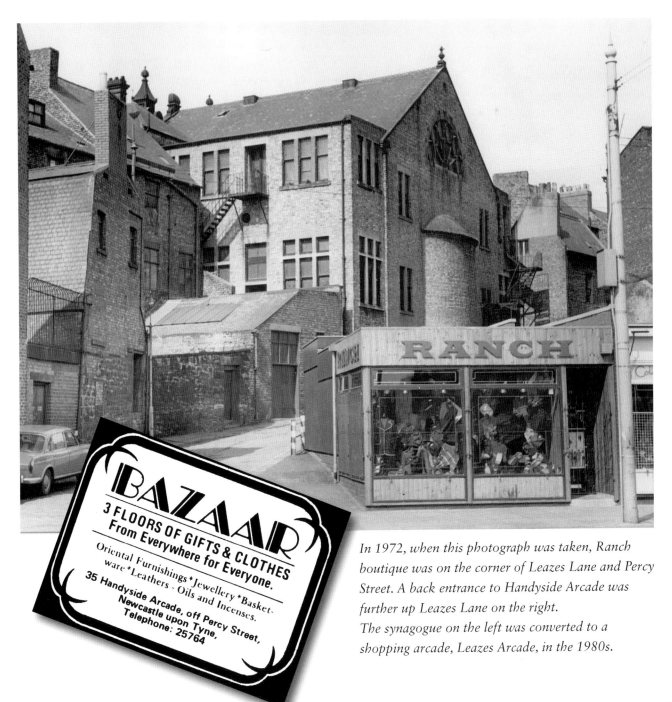

In 1972, *when this photograph was taken, Ranch boutique was on the corner of Leazes Lane and Percy Street. A back entrance to Handyside Arcade was further up Leazes Lane on the right.*
The synagogue on the left was converted to a shopping arcade, Leazes Arcade, in the 1980s.

BAZAAR

3 FLOORS OF GIFTS & CLOTHES
From Everywhere for Everyone.

Oriental Furnishings *Jewellery *Basket-
ware *Leathers - Oils and Incenses.

35 Handyside Arcade, off Percy Street,
Newcastle upon Tyne,
Telephone: 25764

Dreaming ... Eldon Square

Shopping trips involved holding hands and never straying too far from Mam. These visits were occasional and had a purpose. We were usually looking for clothes and Christmas presents.

In the days before Metro we'd drive to Gateshead and park under the railway bridge then cross the road and catch a Newcastle-bound bus on the Tyne Bridge to Worswick Street bus station.

My favourite shop was Fenwick's, and Christmas was my favourite time. I'd coo at the famous window display and fizz with excitement in the toy department. I loved visiting the third floor and remember standing in front of the Sindy dolls wrinkling my nose like Tabitha from *Bewitched* and willing those toys back to my bedroom!

Trips to Fenwick's loo offered me insight into the adult world. Passing Johann's Coffee Shop and the Majorca Café en route to the toilets upstairs, I'd catch glimpses of women through the partition walls chatting over coffee and cake. Would I arrange to meet friends or Mam here in the future?

In the Ladies' Powder Room, I tuned in to the female conversation around me. As I washed my hands I wondered if my adult life would have to be as complicated as the biographies broadcasting in stereo from toilet cubicles. I can still smell that cloying mix of tobacco and perfume in the air as women sorted out their hair, makeup and love lives in front of those big mirrors.

Bainbridge's space-age café in Eldon Square, 1976. It was a great treat for many 1970s kids, though coffee cost a staggering 50p.

On one shopping trip Mam and I went in search of that year's Christmas party dress and ended up in Richard Shops on Northumberland Street. When the shop assistant asked what we were looking for I declared I wanted a dress like 'Anfea'. Mam had to explain that my role model at this time was Bruce Forsyth's second wife and *Generation Game* co-presenter, Anthea Redfern.

After the Queen opened Eldon Square shopping centre our visits to Newcastle were never the same. From 1977 until I hit my teens every trip into town had to include a walk past Bainbridge's space age yellow café and a play on the oversized pencils. Who needed Saltwell Park when Eldon Square offered year-round entertainment for all the family?

Elaine Cusack

Northumberland Street, September 1978.
Mam and I shopped in Binns and Farnons but spent most of our time in and around busy Northumberland Street.
This noisy road had its own theme tune composed of bus engines and brakes, the blind accordion player's tunes
and Evening Chronicle newspaper sellers croaking and yelping like toads and wounded dogs. (Elaine Cusack)

September 1976. A photo-opportunity as Bainbridge staff apparently move stock from the Market Street store past Timpson Shoes along Grainger Street to new premises in Eldon Square.

The Air that I Breathe ... staying local

We had a Co-op van and one other independent grocer who drove around the estate at set times or parked up near the main road to sell groceries. It was handy in the early 70s when maybe one or two cars in the street was the norm. The Co-op was the place to buy almost everything. They paid a dividend on purchases, you had to let them know your 'divi' number and keep your receipts to get cash back. I still remember my mother's, it was 4281.

Dale Toothill

My earliest shopping memories are of going to the 'top shops' for my Nanna. The top shops were on Armstrong Road between Woodstock Road and Delaval Road in Scotswood. A state-of-the-art supermarket, the Hadrian, had recently opened. I loved shopping there, armed with my Nanna's shopping tolley to wheel my purchases home.

One item I remember from my Nanna's shopping list was American Tan tights. Buying tights with your groceries was a really new concept.

The top shops had a variety of traditional shops including a grocer who still weighed out butter and sugar.

Talking about sugar, I remember that in the 1970s there was a sugar shortage. Word soon got round in Scotswood that the Hadrian had a stock of sugar, so off I went to get some. My Nanna seemed to be stockpiling sugar and American Tan tights.

Val Taylor

The rear of Parrish's new department store, Shields Road, Byker, 1970. It was not a swish department store, but practical, without the flair of Fenwick.

Cruddas Park, 1971.

In the early 1970s Cruddas Park shopping centre and library were new and modern enough to be quite an attraction. My mother would walk there with me and my five brothers and sisters all the way from Cherryburn Gardens in Fenham on a Saturday morning, moaning and trailing shopping bags and library books. The way home was worse, all the way up Grainger Park Road with the heavy shopping and the new books.

Linda Green

Newcastle was a building site, Eldon Square was under construction as was the Metro. Streets around the construction were boarded up and scaffolding was everywhere. When it was finished we had a 'new town', indoor shopping, the lot, and it was packed. (Dale Toothill)

Above, Blackett Street 1972. Eldon Square has lost two sides, High Friar Lane has vanished along with the YMCA and all of the south side of Blackett Street.

Right, Archbold Terrace, or what was left of it, Jesmond, 1971.

Run for Home

Lindisfarne, 1978

A changing city

Going... going

As a teenager, my biggest recollection of Newcastle in the 70s is the amount of building work going on. From the upheaval caused by the construction of John Dobson Street, the Central Motorway and the Metro to some iconic – and some very much less so – buildings ... not forgetting the 'New' Stand at St James Park, all part of grand development plans which went on hold for 20 years following relegation in 1978. The redevelopment of the 'old' Town Hall site at the bottom of the Bigg Market. Plans for redevelopment of the 'old' Shieldfield goods yard. The demolition of swathes of 'old' houses, ready for more redevelopment, with everybody appearing to move to new housing estates in either Cramlington or Washington.

Roland Finch

The construction of the Eldon Square shopping centre changed Newcastle. This is a view from a vanishing Prudhoe Street towards Northumberland Street in 1972.

Gone...

In 1973 Newcastle's old Town Hall was finally demolished, its role taken over by the new Civic Centre on Barras Bridge.

It used to be at the bottom of the Bigg Market overlooking the Cathedral and by the 1960s was being used for shows and exhibitions and bizarrely as a winter zoo.

Pulling down the Town Hall opened up the view from the Bigg Market down to the cathedral. The view could never have been photographed before.

Geoff Laws

Above, the Bigg Market in 1971-2, before the Town Hall came down.

Right, 1973, an empty Bigg Market before the construction of the office block that would replace the old Town Hall. Beside the toilets is one of the last remaining blue police boxes where bobbies on the beat could call up HQ.

In 1972 a building that came to stand for all that was worst in the 'brutalist' architecture of the 1970s, and would become one of Britain's most hated buildings, was taking shape on Westgate Road. Westgate House heralded in City News, right, in July 1970, and below in 1972, would span and darken Westgate Road for decades to come.

On the upside, many of Newcastle's finest buildings were being cleaned of the grime of centuries, thanks to a generous government grant.

John Dobson Street was opened (right) on 6 May 1970 by Councillor Neville Trotter, Chairman of the Traffic, Highways and Transport Committee. There was a parade of veteran cars headed by the Lord Mayor's coach. Bewick Court, which was rising beside the Central Library (below) was topped out in January 1971.

By 1975 Newcastle was building thousands of new homes but cracks had been found in several of the new blocks of flats.

Bus Inspectors' cabins like the one below were a feature of the 1970s.

My first car, bought in 1972 for £250 from Ace Motors, Sandyford, was a green Morris Minor. No seatbelts, no heating, no music, just freedom. (Anna Flowers)

Above, the view from Bewick Court, 18 April, 1973. Durant Road curves through the devastation towards New Bridge Street. In the distance are the remains of the New Bridge Street goods yard.

Right, the opening of the Central Motorway East at Brandling Park, 12 August 1975.

2-4-6-8 motorway

Tom Robinson Band, 1977

Across the City

Cars

I passed my test on April Fools Day 1971. My brother had already passed and we shared a forest green Hillman Imp, which was a great little car apart from the braking system, which left a lot to be desired. However, the main cause for concern was that it used to get very overheated. My brother, who was much more into cars than I was, spent a lot of time and money fitting a vinyl roof covering, tinted windows, bucket seats and best of all a radio. Much later on I remember getting an eight-track cassette machine fitted in a mini. I was told it was the future of aural pleasure but it disappeared from the shops within months, then getting hold of these huge cartridges to play on it was almost impossible.

Mik Richardson

Newgate Street, November 1972. The new car park is going up to the left and the new Green Market will occupy the waste ground within a couple of years. The buildings of Blackett Street, beyond, are coming down.

The Central Motorway East, near the junction with Jesmond Road, at its opening on 12 August 1975 as the ribbon is about to be cut. There had been many protests in the Jesmond area about the demolition of Victoria Square in the years leading up to completion of the scheme.

The 70s was when I learned to drive at the BSM on Ridley Place. In those days they had state-of-the-art dual control in the cars. They were also the years when platform soles were all the rage. My instructor was only 5ft 4ins tall, so was well into four-inch heels. I remember driving down by the old Quayside and putting my foot on the brake. It didn't work. The instructor said 'Take your foot off the brake, my platforms are trapped under the duel control brakes,' which goes to show how dangerous these shoes where even when you were not walking on them!

My first car was an Escort L 1100. I was its fourth owner and I was dead proud of it. A lot of cars had letters after their names, GT for example. The L of my Escort stood for Luxury which in the case of this car was a carpet!

Kevin Bell

Buses

I remember smoking being allowed on buses, upstairs on double deckers and at the back on single deck buses. You could catch the bus into town on a Saturday and it took almost an hour to go six miles, a journey that takes about fifteen minutes by car. Some buses still had conductors; they often wore two bags, one carried the ticket dispenser and the other change. How they knew who got on or off I never could figure out, but they rarely missed a fare. If they were upstairs collecting and one person got on they seemed to know exactly who that was and where they sat. We started seeing the old bus notices of 'no spitting' being removed, it was a relic of the old industrial Tyneside where factory workers thought nothing of clearing their throat out even on public transport. We would never dream of taking a taxi.

Dale Toothill

Dennis Astridge

Northumberland Street, 1970. The street was mostly closed to traffic except for buses after the Caller's fire of 1969. It was the start of a better life for pedestrians!

The Worswick Street Dumper

John Mitchell

It was 1974, and the A167M, Central Motorway East was being constructed to allow traffic to bypass the city centre. At this time, Worswick Street bus station, which was behind the Pilgrim Street Police and Fire Stations, was a busy terminus. Thursday, Friday and Saturday nights, between ten and eleven, saw hundreds of late-night revellers pour into the street to catch their last bus. Fights and drunken and disorderly behaviour were commonplace as people crowded onto the platforms and buses.

It was about 10.30pm on a dark, cold, night. I was twenty-one years old and a young copper in his first year. I was with an older colleague who was showing me the ropes.

As we stood there I heard a strange engine noise which I recognised straightaway as coming from a building site 'dumper'. I couldn't actually see it for the crowds of people in the road. It was coming up Worswick Street from the motorway construction site. I realised that it was probably being stolen. As the engine noise got louder, the Red Sea of revellers parted as they scurried out of its path. The front bucket of the dumper emerged and the young tearaway at the wheel drove straight at me as I signalled for him to stop. I was forced to jump to safety and then noticed the wry smile of my older and wiser colleague as he offered to hold my cap while I gave chase!

The unlit dumper drove out across Pilgrim Street and then towards Grey Street. I ran and jumped on the back of the dumper. I clambered across the rear-mounted engine in an attempt to grab the driver. This was great entertainment for the passing crowds. The tearaway was just ignoring my pleas for him to stop. When I was just about to grab him, he jumped off. By this time we were crossing the junction at the Theatre Royal and the driverless dumper was heading straight on. What to do? Let the tearaway get away or stay with the dumper?

I chose the tearaway as I reasoned that the uphill gradient would cause the dumper to stall and stop. I then jumped off the back of the moving dumper and gave chase. A well-timed rugby tackle brought the chase to a close. It also brought a loud cheer from the 'homeward bound' and gave them something to remember about that particular night 'Oot on the Toon'.

However, the grand finale was when I brought my arrest back up to the junction where he had jumped off the dumper. Unfortunately, it had not cut out. It was still running and battering huge dents into the side of a parked car. Oh well, some you win, some you lose.

John Mitchell

The Metro

1974 saw a major shake-up of local government, with some of the smaller urban districts amalgamated into the councils we know today: Newcastle, Gateshead, Sunderland, North and South Tyneside. Tyne and Wear County Council was also created and lasted until 1986 when Mrs Thatcher's government abolished the metropolitan counties. Tyne and Wear was a new authority with overall planning and development powers, including transport planning for the whole area. My father, Rowly Scott-Batey became first Chair of both the new County Council and the Passenger Transport Authority. One of their purposes was 'to help provide for the travel needs of all sections of the community by creating a more attractive integrated transportation system'. The Authority set out to 'own and operate reliable and attractive public transport and ensure that the Metro system is in operation throughout the county at the earliest possible time'.

In the 1970s car ownership in the North East was very low with only around thirty per cent of households having their own transport. It was Rowly's vision that people should be able to travel around the county on clean, efficient, speedy and cheap public transport. The PTA began work on the first modern light rail system in Britain, which became Tyne and Wear Metro. The process was long and complicated, with many meetings in smoke-filled rooms, negotiations with the government over funding for the system, with the trade unions over staffing and pay, and with manufacturers, Metro Camell, over the supply of the unique rolling stock.

The system used 45km of British Rail lines, some disused, and 13km of new track was added, including a 6.1km underground section through central Newcastle and Gateshead. This combination of old railway lines and new track was pioneering at the time. The idea was to create an integrated public transport system, with buses or cars bringing people on shorter journeys to transport interchanges at Heworth, Gateshead, Four Lane Ends and Regent Centre.

During the development a test track in North Tyneside was used, now the North Tyneside Railway, part of the Stephenson Railway

Nexus

The Metro explains itself at the Haymarket bus station, 1975.

Monument Metro Station under construction, 1977. Work began on underpinning the monument in 1975. The giant green barriers were bad news for the businesses at the top of Grainger Street.

Museum. My son got a certificate to say he drove a metro on the test track, although he was only four at the time. A control centre was built at South Gosforth with the latest technology in signalling and real-time information.

The tunnel construction took place over several years and caused tremendous disruption in Newcastle City Centre, particularly around the Monument and at the end of Sandyford Road near the Civic Centre, where there were big holes in the ground.

The process of driving the political side of the development took its toll on my father's health, despite his experience of project management. He suffered as a result of the stress, late nights, and the opposition and obstruction from some quarters. Sadly he died early in 1980, a few months before the first stage of the metro system opened, between Tynemouth and Haymarket, via the coast. My mother, Jessie, opened this phase on 11 August 1980, and had the first ticket. There's a plaque in Haymarket Metro to commemorate the event. The opening was international news and several cities around the world set out to imitate the Metro's innovative technology.

Fiona Clarke

1977. The building of the Metro caused massive disruption to traffic, and to the portico at the Central Station. It was restored in 1979.

A very big hole

In the early 1970s I was working at the University Theatre on Barras Bridge, and I'd walk there along Jesmond Road, a beautiful Victorian Terrace that took me just north of the theatre. Much of the city was being knocked down for 'improvements' including the building of the new motorway that started at the bottom of the Town Moor, and required the demolition of many of the houses at the western end of Jesmond Road, the end nearest the city centre.

Each day on my walk I'd find more and more desolation and destruction.

My working hours meant that I often walked home after dark. One evening I was taking my usual route, heading north from the theatre towards the end of Jesmond Road and then onwards to where it crossed Osborne Road. But things were not quite as they should have been! During the day a huge convoy of diggers had been clearing a massive opening in the ground, which was the beginning of the motorway underpass. The whole of the western end of Jesmond Road had disappeared, and with it, my usual route home!

I didn't see any signs that warned me of the hole. Perhaps because the route was already closed to road traffic, no one thought there would be a mad pedestrian still using it to walk home. Suddenly I found myself poised above a sheer drop which felt like the Grand Canyon. I managed to step back and the next day in full daylight I could see how close I was to meeting my doom! I was just glad to be alive.

Lesley Oakden

The North Road near Jesmond Road, 1 June 1973.

Tyneside Street Press

Above, Newcastle University students demonstrate against the cuts, 1976.

Opposite, the Civic Centre, 1970. (Dennis Astridge)

No More Heroes

The Stranglers, 1977

Politics and Protests

Dirty deeds (done dirt cheap): T. Dan Smith and the Poulson Affair

The man who dominated Newcastle's politics and had extraordinary ambitions for the city was to spend most of the decade that saw some of his dreams become a reality behind bars.

Wallsend-born former Communist T. Dan Smith had become leader of Newcastle's Labour-controlled City Council in 1960, bringing to the job a powerful, charismatic personality and an ambition to drag Newcastle out of the nineteenth century. He aimed to make it the outstanding provincial city in the country and talked in grandiloquent terms of a city 'in the image of Athens, Florence and Rome' and 'the Brasilia of the North' in a reference to the modernist capital the Brazilians had built for themselves. The vision encompassed a spanking new Civic Centre to replace the mouldering old Town Hall, high rise flats to house people cleared from demolished slums and a revitalised city centre with a network of roads slashing through the sky, leaving pedestrians occupying ground-level.

In the 1970s, much of this – for better or for worse – became a reality. But Smith's political career went into freefall when he became embroiled in a massive corruption scandal. Smith – a painter and decorator by trade – had started a public relations company to spread his ambitions nationwide. It soon began to win contracts. One of these led to T. Dan's first brush with the law. In 1970, he was charged with bribery over a redevelopment scheme in Wandsworth. Although acquitted in 1971, he was obliged to resign from politics. Worse was to come.

In 1972, a prominent Yorkshire architect, John Poulson, with whom Smith did business, was undergoing bankruptcy proceedings. The case revealed a network of dodgy deals and bribery. Smith's name came up several times.

The following year, Smith was arrested on corruption charges. In 1974, he pleaded guilty on the grounds, he later said, of sparing friends and family the impact of a trial.

So even as his 'Brasilia' started to take shape on the banks of the Tyne, he languished in gaol. Released in 1977, he was denied membership of the Labour Party and devoted himself, instead, to campaigning for the rights of released prisoners via the Howard League for Penal Reform.

When he died in 1993, his funeral was attended by a large number of politicians and senior officers from the Civic Centre. I asked one how T. Dan Smith should be remembered. 'By the city we live in,' he replied. 'It might not be Brasilia, but it's a lot better than it was.'

Dick Godfrey

Newcastle's transformation from a bombed out, post-industrial ruin into a modern thriving metropolis has been nothing short of remarkable, and it would be fair to say that the principal architect of this metamorphosis was the late T. Dan Smith, who rose from humble circumstances to become a major force in local politics.

Dan was also a well known character in the sleepy little suburb of Newcastle, Spital Tongues. He lived around the corner from us, in a large and imposing town house in the highly desirable Belle Grove Terrace, and could often be seen tearing up and down the back streets in various top end muscle cars, proudly displaying his personalised number plates, 'Dan 68'.

My father, Jim Hoggins, entered local politics in the early 1970s. From all accounts, he was a good councillor with an ability to talk to the 'man in the street' in a language that he could understand. My father rarely mentioned Dan, and I suspect that there was some considerable animosity between the two men. My father was an ex-Army man who had experienced the Second World

T. Dan Smith on Blackett Street, 1977.

War at first hand, whilst Dan had been a pacifist, a conscientious objector and a former member of the Communist Party.

My father eventually fell foul of some dubious ward boundary changes and, out of office, he turned his back on politics, deeply hurt by this apparent public rejection.

T. Dan Smith's meteoric fall from grace has been detailed extensively elsewhere. The charges of corruption, the subsequent court case and his gaol sentence cast a long, dark shadow over the city for many, many years. Though no longer interested in politics, my father still followed the trial with considerable interest. Few came out of the affair smelling of roses.

Released on License in 1977 and, following a number of failed attempts to re-enter politics, Dan effectively retired from public life, and took up residence on the top floor of a block of flats in our village, Mill House.

In the winter of 1977, my father was in charge of a weekly social function for the village's pensioners, the 59 Club, and the atrocious weather meant very few could attend the Club's Christmas Party. My brother and I were press-ganged into distributing a hundred or so Christmas dinners, the majority in the thirteen-storey Mill House.

Starting at ground level, we delivered the lukewarm festive fare to the grateful residents within, most expressing their appreciation with a heartfelt thanks and a Christmas greeting, even if the food was pretty much inedible by then.

Eventually, there was only one name left on our list – Mr. and Mrs T. Dan Smith.

I knocked and waited as footsteps approached. Presently, the door opened.

T. Dan Smith looked old and frail, his worn out eyes set into a sad, lonely face.

'You're Jimmy's boys, aren't you?' he asked, his deep, rich voice still unmistakable.

'Yes,' I replied, somewhat surprised.

'You take after your father,' said the Great Man. 'Stupid.'

He took the food, turned and slammed the door in our faces.

My brother and I just stared at each other, completely bewildered.

Downstairs, I told my father about the exchange. Dad just smiled.

David Hughes

It's different for girls

After I left Live Theatre I got a job as a secretary at the BBC in Newcastle. It was a way for me to get onto that ladder. I threw coffee over one man who tried to touch me up in the office, and was worried I'd lose my job, but in fact men and women actually came up and congratulated me! A friend, one of the only women on the BBC graduate trainee scheme, was given 'girly' jobs to work on, and was treated like dirt. I resented the fact that my salary (£1,765 in 1976) was low compared with what the men got.

Geraldine McClelland

I got my first job in 1976. I worked for an insurance company where there were lots of salesman who thought they had every right to put their arms around you or put their hands on your backside. One even kissed one of the girls. You just had to put up with it.

Angela Sutherland

High Bridge, 1970. Women were still encountering many NO ENTRY signs after the Sex Discrimination Act of 1975.

Children of the revolution

In 1974 I attended a women's consciousness-raising group that met in an upstairs room on Jesmond Road. The right-on women that ran the group thought I was a bit of a lost cause as I was married, and a woman needs a man like a fish needs a bicycle after all, but there was no question of me living with my boyfriend ... we had to be married if we were going to live in the same city as our parents. I hated the fact that you couldn't walk past a building site in Newcastle without being leered at. I bought *Spare Rib* magazine, sometimes from Cradlewell Books, from the first issue. Who wouldn't be a feminist?

Anna Flowers

We went into the Grapes pub because they didn't allow women, just to make a feminist statement, but it was really grotty and very smoky so we didn't make a habit of it! The old men grumbled but we weren't thrown out.

Angela Williams

Motorway protests

Tyneside Environmental Concern (TEC) started out as a Jesmond environmental awareness group. It was self-funding (we collected newspapers and recycled them and ran a home insulation service with government grants) and as a force for the environment, was at least thirty years ahead of its time.

Of the many cultural, musical, entertainment and sporting ventures that I got involved with TEC is the one that fills me with most pride. It was a small group of ex-university types (well, that's Jesmond) with the ability and connections to call upon innumerable reinforcements.

But the apotheosis of TEC's work for me was taking on the City Council, County Council and the Government and defeating the appalling plan to sink the urban motorway through Jesmond creating a massive chasm and taking out swathes of (happily now protected) buildings including parts of Brandling Park, Archbold Terrace and Jesmond Cemetery. The listing of architecturally important buildings was not statutory in the early 1970s.

The plan was to sweep the fast moving traffic straight to the Coast majestically across the Tyne Bridge to ... ? Well! There was the first flaw.

There were many other objectors to the plans including vicars, community groups, 'rent an anarchist', and old ladies who simply wanted to walk their dogs in peace.

The inspector chosen for the final enquiry (late 1973) had never done one before. Although he was a fine, decent man, his inexperience played into our hands. Three days had been set aside for the enquiry: we were off!

The TEC Grand Plan was very simple. Once we took the stand we would filibuster – not a technique that is common in UK politics. To put it simply we would talk and talk and talk – all the time appearing to raise valid technical health- or research-based objections. Our gamble was that eventually the exasperated inspector would overrule us, in which case we would thank him and walk away. He had no authority to decide what was admissible or not in his terms of reference and therefore the enquiry would be invalid.

Of course everyone fell for it.

One of the TEC team spoke for three-and-a-half hours on the dangers of particulates from diesel traction, several times ticking off the QCs for interrupting him. Another boomed

Tim Callaghan

Cradlewell Books, 235 Jesmond Road, 1977. The Socialist Centre was here from the mid-1970s holding political meetings, talks, and arts events. It advertised in Tyneside Street Press, an alternative newspaper that ran from May 1976 to December 1977. Days of Hope bookshop opened on Westgate Road in 1979.

along from one day to the next on severance and its deleterious effects upon the aged – the QCs remained remarkably quiet!

We gave them public service versus private car data in layer after interminable layer ... and then with lunch approaching on the final day, the angry roars never abating, the inspector faltered – with the immortal words of 'I've heard enough of this, I will take no more of your evidence.'

GAME SET MATCH

We thanked him and I apologised to the room for not being able to present our final four days' evidence. It got a laugh ... but actually was true. So the enquiry drew to a close. The findings were that the motorway would go ahead as planned. This prompted an objection and legal challenge from William Duffy, representing TEC. The Law Lords ruled that the enquiry was null and void. Another enquiry would have to be set. Within a short space of time, the listing of buildings became the norm, the Government ran out of money

Alternative newspaper Muther Grumble for June 1972, records an anti-motorway demonstration that took place near the ruins of Victoria Square in May. There was a brief sit-in on St Mary's Place.

and the councils had lost the will to keep going. That's why you have strange truncated fly offs and the cemetery and many fine Victorian buildings are still intact. Apart from my lovely kids, it's the thing I'm most proud of.

Andy Hudson

Planner for the people

Coming to Newcastle in Newcastle in 1971, a fresh faced postgraduate from Glasgow University's Town and Regional Planning department, to work for the Young Volunteer Force Foundation, was like a dream come true. Years earlier I'd been inspired to become a town planner by a TV programme about T. Dan Smith and his 'Brasilia of the North'. By now, of course, he had been discredited. But I was still fired with revolutionary enthusiasm, inspired by movements across the world, and optimistic that we could change things.

I quickly established myself in the West End of Newcastle. I was going to be a 'Planner for the People'. This was a time when planning was coming in for severe criticism because of the inhumane way it had broken up working-class communities and put them in out-of-town suburbs with few facilities or in huge, cheaply-built tower blocks.

West End Tenants' Association was already doing trailblazing work in the slum clearance areas of Elswick, campaigning for local residents to be given the opportunity to move in groups with their friends and neighbours into nearby new housing that they would help design. Sadly this never happened, but the council suggested that residents in nearby Arthur's Hill could be given the opportunity instead. At last my chance had come!

I quickly arranged street meetings in people's homes, where residents could work with planners and architects, helping to design the new estate they would move to and choose the neighbours they would live next to. Local people became strong community activists, formed their own committee, opened and ran their own advice centre, campaigned to try to maintain decent environmental conditions, produced a community newspaper and information sheets, all designed to protect and reassure local residents. An adventure playground and summer playscheme were

Phil Kitchen

established and the very first community festivals in the city were established. We linked up with street theatre companies, such as Live Theatre, Red Ladder and Welfare State International in pubs, clubs and on the streets.

In the East End, similar things were happening, most notably in Byker. The new estate has become world renowned in the architectural field, though the Byker Wall has always remained controversial amongst local residents. Byker also spawned many community groups involved in a range of campaigning and cultural activities and had its own community magazine, the *Byker Phoenix*.

Community workers and activists

Stanhope Street Action Area Community Shop, 1972.

networked across the city, holding joint meetings and conferences. A Joint Clearance Areas Action Group and a Newcastle Tenants' Federation were established to formalize solidarity. Links were made with the National Tenants' Organisation and the local Trades Council. We would go on May Day demonstrations and rub shoulders with lefties in the Days of Hope (known by some, quite unfairly, as 'Haze of Dope') bookshop at the bottom of Westgate Hill. And of course you had to show your left wing credentials by attending the Annual Dance for Peace and Socialism held at the Guildhall.

We hoped this would be the start of a revolution, in which people from disadvantaged working class communities, trade unionists and sympathetic trained professionals from all over the country would come together in solidarity to form a more just and equal society? It hasn't happened, has it? ... Yet.

Phil Kitchen

Money: going decimal

All banks were closed for two days before 'D-Day' (15 February 1971). Most high-street shops opted to go decimal from day one and all their sales tickets were dual priced. However, the barrow-boys and street traders were, as ever, a law unto themselves and continued to price and sell in £-s-d for some considerable time after the official transition period. All shops displayed a government issue chart listing £-s-d prices alongside their decimal equivalents and a number of 'easy' conversion formulae were published. A popular one was to halve the price in shillings and pence to get the price in decimal eg: 10s = 100 = 50p; 3s-6d = 36 = 18p. Decimalisation meant that 'tanner', 'two bob', 'florin', and 'threepenny bit' were lost from everyday language. The 'new halfpenny' was withdrawn from circulation some ten years later. Pensioners found it a bit difficult to adjust to the new system but school children suddenly found life a whole lot easier and one survey suggested that only about ten per cent of those questioned thought that they had been 'ripped off'.

Michael Landon

Freemans, Bigg Market, displays prices in old and new money in 1971.

Just before decimalisation, the new 50p pieces were in circulation while the ten-bob note was still in use. I had 10s 4d in my pocket and popped into Fenwicks for a magazine. As I went in I tossed a penny to the blind accordion player who always stood outside. When I went to pay I realised that what I thought was a penny had in fact been a 50p coin! That was a serious amount of money (remember beer was only a shilling per pint). I dashed back out but the beggar wasn't blind after all, as he'd legged it!

Dan Kantorowich

Winters of discontent: The three-day weeks,1972 and 1974

On the 9th February, 1972, with NUM miners on strike, a state of emergency was declared by PM Edward Heath and two days later, the three-day working week was introduced to save electricity. On 31 December 1973 history repeated itself with another miners' strike and three-day week.

I remember the power cuts and three day week of February 1972. We were living in Molineux Court flats in Heaton. From our vantage point on the seventh floor you could see the city in darkness. With no power for the lift it was a long walk up the stairs for anyone who got caught out, especially residents on the 14th floor. My dad was an overhead crane driver at C.A. Parsons heavy engineering where at that time it was said 'you could always get a job'. Everyone had to stock up on candles, my elder brother Lance tried making homemade candles out of cooking fat and although they worked to an extent, our mum complained the flat smelled like a chippie. For me at 11 years old it was exciting living by candle light for a few hours a night. Dad bought a small camping GAZ stove to boil water. It was around this time we rented our first colour set from Radio Rentals but there was often no television. It was almost a step back in time as we listened to the radio, which put on special programmes, including a nightly ghost story read by Vincent Price. We also played cards.

Brian Thompson

To save electricity the domestic power supply was cut for a six-hour period each day. This changed every three days and timetables were published in the local press. Electric appliances such as washing machines, cookers and vacuum cleaners could not be used without power so domestic routines had to be re-organised. Our ancient central heating system was gas fired, with a clockwork timer and a gravity feed: we used a gas cooker and there was a gas fire in the lounge, so apart from using candles and a camping gas light when necessary, we were not badly affected by the power cuts. A neighbour borrowed our camping gas stove so that she could boil a kettle if the power was 'off' at breakfast time. If your house happened to be in an electricity supply sector that included some essential service such as a hospital, then your supply was probably maintained as normal. One 'deprivation' that no-one escaped – all TV transmissions stopped at 10.30pm each evening, but I do not recall that many people thought that this was any great loss! Industry was of course the main target and badly hit. Not only did they

Parsons Engineering, Heaton, was hit by the power cuts.

regularly lose their power supply like everybody else but they were not allowed to work overtime to compensate for lost production. Restaurants, food shops and news organisations were exempt. Many shops maintained some sort of service using portable gas lights and the small corner shop probably found this easier to do than the big high street multiples. It was possible to obtain exemption from the power cuts if a company could establish that they performed some vital service. At work (the RVI Newcastle) we got pleas from several of our laboratory suppliers asking us to support their application for such an exemption. As I remember, none were successful. The hospital itself had a couple of generators 'on standby' to provide an emergency power supply if necessary.

Michael Landon

At the time of the three-day-week I was working in the drawing office of a steel fabrication company, which was diversifying from manufacturing coal handling plant into building products, particularly pressed steel lintels and up and over garage doors for all the new housing that was being built by the likes of William Leech and Bellway. The raw material for lintels was bought in in rolls at the required widths at ⅛ or 3/16 inch thicknesses. Because of the industrial unrest the buyer could not obtain these rolls so he resorted to buying large steel plates and I had to do a kind of jigsaw puzzle in reverse to work out the best way to cut them up to meet our orders.

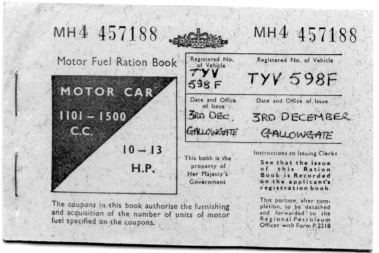

The oil crisis of 1973 along with the miners' strike prompted the government to issue petrol ration books. In the end they were never used. The winter was mild, coal stocks lasted. Edward Heath lost the election in February 1974.

The workshops could not function without power for welding, galvanising, overhead cranes etc, but a large part of the office could, as long as they could see. Accounts used comptometers – mechanical adding machines – there were no computers – and the phones would work as would mechanical typewriters. I had the use of a battery electronic calculator, quite compact, about an inch thick with a neon type display which cost about £85 – my weekly wage was £24!

The government announced that fuel rationing was imminent and I still have some coupons which were issued in preparation by the Ministry of Power though never required. I suspect they were left over from the war.

Nic Grant

Bomb threats

After the Post Office Tower bomb of 1971 and the pub bombings of 1974, a couple of times a term a man with an Irish accent would phone the school to warn the headmaster that there was a bomb in the building. The fire alarm would ring and we would all troop down to the playing field where we stood shivering. We welcomed the break from lessons. Who didn't dream of blowing up the school?

I was still dealing with bomb threats when I joined the Civil Service in my first full-time job. Letter bombs had been sent to lots of government buildings and in my office, I was the one that opened the post. Beside the post table there was a helpful list of clues that could indicate an item of mail that was really a bomb. I was so keen not to have a hand blown off that I learned these by heart. I can still remember them. The first thing to look for was an Irish postmark. A

Singers at the Quayside Sunday Market, 1974.

packet that was unusually heavy for its size was suspect, as was one that was unbalanced. Pin-sized holes in the envelope, greasy stains and the smell of almonds were all danger signs.

Vanessa Histon

The ghost County Council

We still refer to Tyne and Wear, although its County Council only lasted a few years, from 1974 until 1986. Its headquarters was in Archbold Terrace, and it covered Newcastle, Gateshead, Sunderland, North and South Tyneside, which had previously been districts of either Northumberland or Durham. While the five Metropolitan Boroughs took power over most local services, the County Council dealt with strategic planning and transport. Its ghost survives in Tyne and Wear-wide organisations, such as Nexus and Tyne and Wear Archive & Museums Service, and its most notable achievement was the development of the Metro system.

Fiona Clarke

Georgia On My Mind: President Carter and The Friendship Force

The friendship force originated in Atlanta, Georgia. Local newscasters, including Mike Neville, switched positions with the Yanks and we had our local news presented by the Americans for a week or two. An American cop was also on duty directing traffic in Newcastle. That must have been quite a sight.

Dale Toothill

I was studying graphic design at Newcastle Polytechnic when US President Jimmy Carter visited the North East on 6 May, 1977. I remember being let inside an inner cordon by security, they must have thought I was a professional photographer. I stood in front of a small TV tower and had a great view. I must have been about 50ft or so from the President. I had borrowed a 35mm Pentax, and a light meter from our Photography Dept with the aim of recording this auspicious day, just two days before my 19th birthday. I then developed and printed them myself in our dark room.

Tim Callaghan

The President spoke at 10.30am after flying in from the Airport by helicopter. He was presented with the honorary freedom of the city by Councillor Hugh White, Lord Mayor of Newcastle, watched by Prime Minister Jim Callaghan.

On 6 May 1977, US President Jimmy Carter visited Newcastle. The President shouted 'Haway the lads!' and the crowd went wild. So many people crowded onto the area in front of the Civic Centre on St Mary's Place that there was subsidence where the hidden Pandon Burn flows underground on its way to the Tyne.

The Newcastle upon Tyne Friendship Force Club participated in the very first Friendship Force exchange with Atlanta on 4 July 1977 when 381 Ambassadors flew to the USA, and 381 American Ambassadors returned to Newcastle. See page 214 for another story about the Friendship Force.

It was 1970, and there was a bit of tomfoolery going on outside the Civic Centre. Needless to say, he didn't actually do it. He does something important with the European Parliament now.

Dennis Astridge

Opposite, Newcastle University, September 1971.

School's Out!

Alice Cooper, 1972

The sit-in: homes not offices

I was extensively involved (by accident) in what started as a student sit in and protest in a building called Cuthbert House – a brand new uninhabited office block in the middle of Newcastle. The protest was organised by some Social Science students linked to a number of political activists and was intended to highlight the plight of the homeless. I ran the Social Science football team and found out about the protest when I learned that we would be unable to field a side in the Wednesday intra mural league because most of the team would be in the squat. Those who knew about these things gained entry to the building on Sunday afternoon and I went along with my mates on the Sunday evening.

What I didn't know was that it had been widely publicised in the Student Union and it had been hijacked by well over 100 students having a party in the office block! A good time was had by all and I remember that on the Monday morning it dawned on everyone that there was no sanitation and no running water and conditions had become grim very quickly.

We were on TV and in the papers, a colliery brass band came out one night to support us (and brought crates of beer and boxes of crisps), people fell out, there were fights. By Tuesday or Wednesday most people had left, but we had been joined by real homeless people, including a young couple with two babies. It was all very sad. We talked through partially open doors to council officials and the building's owners.

Eventually by Friday there were about six of us students left. I'm not sure exactly how, but an empty house near the General Hospital was found and established as a place for the young family to go and – with full co-operation from the police and joined by the local Trades Council – we marched out of the building and through Newcastle City Centre on the Saturday afternoon.

I remember the date vividly – Saturday 6 March 1974. The day that Newcastle beat Notts Forest 4-3 in the cup. There was a pitch invasion and the FA ordered the game to be replayed. While all that was going on we put the family in the house and went home. I had a bath and slept forever!

John Williams (Ncle 1973-76)

Courier immortalises the 1974 sit-in.

I spent a fair amount of time in the Union drifting from one bar to another. Friday and Saturday nights especially meant starting off in the lower bars and working upwards until you ended up at Level 6 disco. A bonus with the Union was that the Long Bar down in the refectory opened at 4pm, so if you lingered with a pint when the Mens Bar shut at 3pm you could then wander down to the Long Bar to be ready for it opening.

Roger Shaw (Ncle 1974-77)

Dennis Astridge

1973 demonstration against proposed changes to student grants.

Chris Mabbott

In the early 70s I lived in a student flat in a cul-de-sac off Westgate Road. It was idyllic. Absolutely scruffy. Just what a student needed. When you banged the table, little things would wriggle out of the cracks in the wood, squirm around for a bit and then disappear back down the cracks. We didn't mind.

One thing we Hairies had to watch for were skinheads. Once, returning to the flat after a night at the Union there was a mini Skinhead riot on Westgate Road. A couple of dozen were kicking hell out of each other, throwing glasses and bottles. We crept quietly past, pressing ourselves against the walls hoping we'd be unobserved. As soon as we reached the post office we ran down the alley that led to our flat. You couldn't hear the yelling and the swearing. All that violence a few yards away and we were in a peaceful oasis that overlooked the river. Happy days. It was a very safe flat as the police often parked outside (they suspected us of smoking more than cigarettes).

Chris Mabbott (Ncle 1969-72)

There were some difficult times in the 1970s, culminating in the winter of discontent, pickets outside factories and garbage in the streets. Student houses were eye-opening – several we looked at had no inside toilet and landlords openly stated that a group of male students was not what they wanted. Eventually we found an Addams Family monstrosity of a house on Westgate Road. We made the most of it and had a fantastic time living

Dennis Astridge

February 1970, Simonside Terrace, Heaton. We were second-year Town and Country Planning students about to set off for a traffic survey in Blyth. The survey was clearly pointless in the deep snow, but we went anyway. (Dennis Astridge, Ncle 1968-1973)

there. We even joined in with the locals for a Jubilee street party – but the memories of this are a little hazy!

The power cuts of 1977 sometimes made studying in our house a challenge. The old houses up Stanhope Street were being demolished and cleared and the walk home from lectures often involved picking up some wood to burn on our open kitchen fire – around which we sat in the dark, cooked toast, talked and sang – thinking we were living in the 1930s rather than the 1970s!

When we graduated we had a party in a room above the New Darnell and then back at our house, where a policeman knocked on the door at 2am and was promptly asked by one of my parents if he knew the second verse of *The Blaydon Races*.

David Clarkson (Ncle 1975-78)

The big chill

Well, it was cold, oh so cold. In my first year I lived in Havelock Hall. I remember storing the free milk from the University farm on the window sill, only for it to be nicked by the neighbour below by deft use of a hooked stick. We were always setting fire to the Baby Bellings by forgetting the toast.

Our later flat was over a convenience store on the corner of Jesmond Road and Osborne Avenue. It was the scene of memorable parties; during one, the ceiling came down!

Dan Kantorowich

In December 1970 it snowed so much that we built an igloo in the Quad and four of us slept in it over night. We got our pictures in the *Evening Chronicle* and I was quoted as saying it was warmer than our flat, which was absolutely true.

My weekly budget was £5 (to cover food, books, clothes, etc.). We used to buy cheap ex-army stuff from a shop just on the town side of the Byker Bridge. I bought myself a bike from a shop on Raby Street in Byker for 10s 6p, great investment. I used to cycle everywhere and once was blown flat over riding up John Dobson Street carrying an A1 portfolio under one arm. All the motorists thought it hilarious.

Dan Kantorowich (Ncle 1969-75)

In my second year, 1977-1978, I shared an unheated house with several others in Cowgate. That winter it was so cold that the toilet froze in the house and we all gave up trying to use the bathroom there, it was so icy! Thankfully there was a fantastic facility in the basement of the Student Union building. For a very small fee, you could have a deep, steamy bath.

Elizabeth Taylor (Ncle 1976-79)

Castle Leazes was one of the first mixed halls of residence, although men and women were meant to be on separate floors! There were occasional formal dining nights when gowns were required. These were helpful in protecting one's only suit from the stray food that flew around until the warden intervened.

Sherry was available before the meal. The sherry was rumoured (never proven though) to be from South Africa, despite students' vocal resistance to apartheid. The junior common room

University of Newcastle/Alan Johnson

Castle Leazes students live it up. Were they dancing to Mungo Jerry in 1976? Or were they rowing to Oops Upside Your Head by the Gap Band, a party favourite of 1979? It doesn't look like they'd remember!

used to organise a film show every Sunday evening, which most of us went to before cocoa and an early night because of 9am lectures on a Monday. The bar only opened for an hour at 9.30pm, but never sold real ale.

Stuart Holliday (Ncle 1968-71)

We didn't worry about healthy food at the time. The standard lunch in the Lower Bun Room in the Union was sliced white bread sandwich with processed cheese slice and raw onion followed by a chocolate cup cake. The bun room was to be avoided on Thursday nights as the agriculture students who met there were very scary!

I remember the powercuts – revising by candlelight in our digs in South Gosforth.

I always lived out. The highlights in Jesmond were the Lonsdale pub and the old fleapit cinema next door, which had films about a month after everywhere else but lots cheaper. The shops at the back of Ashleigh Grove comprised a launderette, off-licence, frozen food shop and a single phone box for those frantic, plaintive calls home before exams.

We went to discos at Henderson Hall, which was all male at that time so we had a lot of fun. At the formal ball there in 1972 the dress code was black tie and long frocks. In my first year there was an all-night 'RAG' (President's Ball) with Ginger Baker, Jack Bruce and Lindisfarne.

Maggie Waller (Ncle 1971-74)

Phil Ireson

Around 5,000 students march against government attempts to curb student union powers, December 1971, although most of the chanting was 'Mrs Thatcher, milk snatcher'. 2000 fitted into the Haymarket Cinema for an address by Vice-Chancellor Henry Miller. There was the usual bomb hoax! (Rod Macleod)

My first memory of Newcastle is arriving on a dark, wet December evening in 1975 to stay overnight for an interview (BSc (Speech)) the following day ... As I got on the train heading south again late the next afternoon, I thought 'Thank goodness I won't have to come here again!' Much to my surprise, I was made a conditional offer, which I kept as second choice. I didn't get the A-level results needed for my first choice university so I had to come back to Newcastle after all.

Student life was a great improvement on school and I soon made new friends ... I don't think I went to bed before 3am any night that first term but this didn't mix well with twenty-five contact hours a week and 9am lectures on four days a week.

The food in Ethel Williams Hall was reckoned to be better than other halls ... Kettles were allowed in bedrooms but there was no fridge (we put milk outside on the window sill in winter) in the kitchen – just sinks and a two-ring Baby Belling hob. Second year meant moving out of hall to one of the new flats built in the grounds of Easton Hall ... warm, clean and unlimited hot water and heat included in the rent. No iced up toilets for us!

We had a new local, the Brandling Arms. We used the local laundrette and bought liquorice bootlaces from the sweetshop to while away the washing time. We could use the swings in Exhibition Park and walk to the Hoppings in June. It was hard to leave at the end of the course. There is nothing to beat the first sight of the Tyne Bridges either from road or rail – it's like coming home to an old friend.

Josephine Scriven (Ncle 1975-1979)

In the first year I lived at Freemans Hall, Castle Leazes, where there was a male to female ratio of about 10:1, so this was a monastic year ... communal eating; table football and television in the common room; trying to dye my first, unsatisfactorily faint moustache with Clairol and instead staining my stainless steel basin an indelible brown; the rolled up towel at the base of my door to stop the smell of dope from pervading the corridor; too many evenings spent in too many bars. The Spital in Hunters Road was one regular haunt, where 'Mr Newcastle' T. Dan Smith could sometimes be found propping up the bar, as the Poulson corruption scandal gathered pace.

Rod McLeod

Living in hall was institutional, unexciting, and gender-segregated ... the walk across the moor through grazing cows was a pleasure to a country boy like me, and on summer afternoons we sometimes played bowls on the greens off Richardson Road, tolerated by the properly dressed players in their white flannels and blazers.

Wings plays Castle Leazes. In February 1972 fellow planner Andy Brack was walking near the campus when a van stopped beside him and Paul McCartney leant out and asked if there was anywhere they could play a gig. Andy said he'd fix it, and so Newcastle was included in Wings' unscheduled 'University Tour'. (Rod Macleod)

The next year I moved to Bayswater Road, Jesmond and shared a house with two other Newcastle students and one from the Poly. I drank in the men-only bar at the Lonsdale, where one pressed a bell-push to summon the waiter for refills. The Brandling and the Collingwood were handily together across a car park. One of my housemates had an aging Austin Cambridge that he ran on a minimal tank of petrol. It regularly ran dry at traffic lights, and he would jump out and pour a pint or so into the tank from a small can he kept in the boot. Every now and then we took off with tents and a primus, and spent a weekend climbing in the Lake District, and sometimes there were outings with the Newcastle and District Beagles.

In the third year I moved to Normanton Terrace, Elswick. This was my first mixed-sex house, and altogether more fun. Normanton Terrace was in a seedy part of Elswick, where the streets behind had been demolished and a boiler-suited flasher terrorised the girls in the house. On one occasion one of the girls answered a knock at the door and a dozen children burst in and tore through the house trying to grab whatever they could. Luckily everyone was in and we frisked and ejected them without losing anything. The local corner shop was run by a friendly, long-haired Pakistani. He kept a two-bar heater on the counter, on which he balanced a tray to cook eggs, with bacon hung over the bars. His chest freezer was an untidy muddle of boxes and unwrapped loose fish. He sold me a crombie coat that had had the labels cut off.

On a minimum grant, this was a hard year. We took turns to queue outside the local baker before opening time each Saturday morning for the reject bread and buns, which they sold off cheaply, and I frequented a tobacconist on the corner of St Thomas's Street that sold cigarettes singly, from a pint mug on the counter. Once, in desperation, we broke up a cupboard to burn in the sitting-room hearth. Things got better when my girlfriend's father, who was a miner in Ashington, offered some coal from his free allowance; we hired a van and collected enough sacks to see us through the winter.

Rod Macleod (Ncle 1970-75)

Dennis Astridge

As planning students we were very aware of the debate surrounding the City's slum clearance programme. This photograph was taken in Elswick in early 1970 for a small exhibition highlighting the problems faced by people still living in the clearance areas. (Dennis Astridge)

I remember that the fact that our union sold more beer than any other student's union (and more than second and third together) was a source of pride. The Level 6 disco and Agrics' night in the union, were weekly highlights. We met for lunch in the Mens Bar. Along with many others we boycotted South African goods and Barclays Bank and sported our anti-Maggie badges.

Highlights at the Mayfair included The Police, ACDC, the Jam, Generation X, and Eddie and the Hotrods. My pride and joy as far as clothes went were my cheesecloth shirts, dungarees and red clogs, and Kickers. My boyfriend wore baseball boots and skinny jeans. Unlike the locals who were always out in just a T-shirt we were wrapped up, most of the time, in our duffle coats and donkey jackets.

Philippa Besant (Ncle 1977-80)

A student from Ceylon

In October 1971, a shy bride in a sari, six yards long, and her groom, board the aircraft from Ceylon, a tiny island smaller than Scotland, for a study-honeymoon at Newcastle University.

It was twilight when we arrived on a cold, wet and windy day. We were stranded as the banks at the airport were closed after dark so we phoned our only contact, Prof. Douglas Wise, Head of the Department of Architecture, and instantly had transport, shelter and food, (including Yorkshire pudding).

We lived in Fern Avenue digs, which meant we could stroll in Jesmond Dene and look at the work of artists on the bridge. We shared a kitchen with the landlord and another Newcastle University student, who, I was convinced, existed solely on large bowls of Kellogg's corn flakes! Rice and curry, our familiar food and a culinary delight today, was only for the bold and adventurous.

At the end of our stay we had a convocation, two degrees BArch (Hons) … and a baby in our arms!

Shiranee Balasuriya (Ncle 1971-73)

Armstrong Bridge craft market, Jesmond, 1970.

The student photographer

I came to Newcastle from York University where I was studying chemistry. I decided to get out and study psychology at Newcastle instead. I discovered I much preferred Newcastle, as the university was in the heart of the city unlike the campus life of York. I also had sufficient spare time to find my true vocation: photography. It was already a hobby in a vague kind of way, but I taught myself from a text book how to develop films and make prints – all black and white – and started doing pictures for *Courier*, the student newspaper.

Working on the paper gave me a grounding in real work as a photographer as I had to photograph meetings, visiting bands, sports matches and the like, which had to be delivered by a deadline, but the strongest incentive was doing the Back Page Spot, where I ran around looking for attractive girls and persuading them to be photographed for this glorious position, which would no doubt lead to greater things. I don't recall finding a real girlfriend through this activity, but it did me no harm.

I lost all the negatives and prints from that time, and to be fair, most of the pictures I made then are fairly dull, however the opportunity of working on the paper and the student magazine sowed the seeds of possibility, and gave me technical and personal confidence to launch a career as a freelance photographer.

Chris Steele-Perkins (Ncle 1967-70)

Chris Steele-Perkins

The Green Market, captured towards the end of its life, 1970.

I'm an Upstart

In 1978 a band from South Shields, Angelic Upstarts, were making a name for themselves in the wake of the death of Liddle Towers, a boxer who had died in police custody in Gateshead in 1976. They were booked to play by Students' Union Entertainments. The vision remains as vivid today as when I witnessed it back then. A horde of punk rockers – hair the colour of traffic lights, faces held together by safety pins, studded, strapped and screaming alongside big haired and flared students. On stage, a frenzied performance from the boys in the band. The token pig's head kicked high into the air, a frenetic audience tossing it from person to person, made an unlikely coalition of students and punks, united in their rage against authority. Standing at the back of the room, wearing a raincoat, carrying a briefcase and brolly, a senior member of the University's administrative staff. His face a study in horror and disbelief – his unspoken thought ... this sort of behaviour could never happen in a British University. Could it?

Angelic Upstarts, 1978.

Rik Walton

Helene Dolder

My last Rag party, 1970

What a night that was! Parties and students were invented so long ago that we forget the hard hard typing through the night on ancient typewriters; the slog of afternoon practicals. I'll never forget the Prof, and the others, and all they did for us in the beautiful, but antiquated Armstrong Building. Who else could get you a Science in Industry Award! Maybe all those old theses we produced are still stored in the walls there somewhere. Perhaps not!

David Armstrong (Ncle 1967-1970)

Phil Ireson

Overland to India

Having completed a degree in Mechanical Engineering at Newcastle University in 1970, and despite not being a natural traveller, I got together with a fellow student to make plans to travel overland to India. After working as labourers on the University Theatre site (no training, no health and safety, driving a dumper truck) and a brief period for Securicor, we purchased an old ambulance – in fact it had been the works ambulance for Clarke Chapman, and though twenty-five years old had only done 5,000 miles. During the summer we set about converting it to take passengers, with the view to setting off in mid-September. One by one, friends that had said they were up for the adventure dropped away, and in the end we had to advertise in the Student's Union. John Wilkinson, later to be more famous as the charismatic guitarist Wilko Johnson with the group Dr Feelgood, signed up. Soon there were seven of us, each contributing £25 and with the 'bus' as ready as it would ever be, we set off for the Hovercraft to Calais. It proved to be very unreliable but managed a thousand miles before it finally broke down in Turkey – the brake pipes had fractured when the bus bottomed out on a rocky road. Against the odds we reached India by December before going our separate ways. Wilko had to be repatriated with hepatitis and without any money. I stayed on, joining up with other travellers in Delhi and Goa, finally flying back on a charter flight in June 1971. As well as the obligatory *Lord of the Rings*, I carried a section of Jack Kerouac's *Dharma Bums* with me around India – strangely, Wilko took the Bible and a postcard of the Mithraeum – he was a fan of Mithras at the time.

Fraser MacKay (Ncle 1967-1970)

Early hours with the Open University

The Open University began and for four years I was a student again. We had to buy a VHF radio and I had to stay up until the early hours to listen to lectures and to watch them on the television. Never academically bright, after four years I ended up with an undistinguished degree but still a degree.

Mike Young

Right, Courier advertises escapes from Newcastle, 1974.

Fabulous Grand Tours from SUNDOWNERS

Overland Adventure Holidays

OVERLAND to KATHMANDU
"The CARAVAN" — 44 Days – £138.00 (incl. accommodation)
"The ALEXANDER" — 72 Days – £168.00
"The SCHEHEREZADE" - 80 Days – £198.00 (incl. Middle East)
Economically priced connecting Travel to all destinations

RUSSIA and EASTERN EUROPE
"The BALALAIKA" — 23 Days – £92.00 (Russia, Poland & Finland)
"The COSSACK" — 42 Days – £152.00 (incl. The Ukraine &
Black Sea)

WESTERN EUROPE
"The EUROPA" — 63 Days – £202.00 (10 countries)
"The GYPSY" — 42 Days – £145.00 (8 countries)

SCANDINAVIA
"The VALKYRIE" — 28 Days – £99.00 (incl. Arctic Circle)

EUROPE and NORTH AFRICA
"The SUNSEEKER" — 63 Days – £212.00 (14 countries)

The JET/SHIP way to AUSTRALIA and NEW ZEALAND from £135.00

Sundowners Travel, 8 Hogarth Place, London SW5. Telephone:
(01) 370 4317, 373 5623. Please send me your free colour brochure
and details of free film show (wine and cheese provided).

NAME

ADDRESS

Public Health sewer staff, outside the Civic Centre, 1975. Apparently no sex discrimination here. The city's sewers were being modernised.

Right, Northumberland Street, 1973. Beyond the re-built Callers is a gap where Van Allan's old premises awaits re-building after the fire of 1969. It was completed in 1975, which also saw the opening of the new British Home Stores and C & A on the corner of Northumberland Street and Northumberland Road.

I Don't Like Mondays!

Boomtown Rats, 1979

Apprenticed in the shipyards

One morning in early August 1972 I joined Hawthorn Leslie Engineers Ltd as an apprentice. The bus ran from Gateshead to Newcastle and then along Walker Road. The buses sometimes came three at a time, filling up with men of all ages and women who worked the canteens or wages departments.

The pungent smell of the shipyards and engineering works filled the air. The welders' overalls were always full of small holes from the sparks and most of the burners had patches on their knees from kneeling to burn plate with oxy-acetylene. Each bus filled up quickly until there was standing room only. I was shocked at the number of people I would have to fight to get on the bus each day but more amazed when they all poured out into the streets to go to work.

The evenings after work were the reverse and the men spilled out like ants from a nest and spread like a thick oil across the streets, each knowing that they had to be first at the stop to get home quickly. Others sauntered off to the local bar for a pint as the battle had been lost at the toot of the works horn and they knew they were too far away from the door to make it.

The confidence of each man was high, they knew their place and skills, they felt vital and important. I worked with men who took drawings and large plates of metal and at the end of the day folded and cut

that metal as if it was paper and made the machines that powered ships around the world. I still remember the smell of the paint cooking on the metallic skin of a 45ft high Sulzer RND firing up on the first day, the thunder of the engine as it vibrated the bedplate fastened to the shop floor, and the satisfaction of each man, including myself. Now there is only St Peter's Basin and its apartments where the works once stood. Sadly, Thatcher came and we all went, and the buses stopped running.

John R. McCallum

Apprentices at Vickers-Armstrong Elswick Works, early 1970s.
When the workers came out after their shift you'd find an Evening Chronicle seller on every corner of Scotswood Road.

Do what you wanna do: jobs for boys and girls

In 1971 I finished my apprenticeship as a ships' draughtsman at Swan Hunter and in doing so was made eligible for the dreaded redundancy list which came round at regular intervals when work was short. I survived two spells on the list without being laid off but it drove me to find a new job in Newcastle City Centre. The job was so different from the shipyards. I worked in compact offices in Dean Street and instead of working with hundreds of people there were just a couple of dozen and no unions either. The real beauty about this job however was the location. There was always something to do in the dinner hour. One of my favourite haunts was the Handyside Arcade which had a second-hand record shop with rows of albums that I happily rummaged through. I was working there during that fantastic summer of 1976. One day it was snowing (local cricket matches were called off), the next day the sun came out in a cloudless sky and remained that way for what seemed like months. People in Newcastle during this time were just stripping off and sunbathing wherever there was a spare piece of grass. It was incredible. I used to drop the car outside of town and walk in, it was such a feel-good time.

Mik Richardson

I worked for the local authority in Regent Centre where queues and queues of impatient people came in to tax their cars. The office was only just going on to computerisation around 1977. We were wary of computers and none of us wanted to use them, knowing that it was quicker to write things down, but we had no choice. They were simple enough for what we had to do, which was printing tax discs. If we got stressed we could just light up a cigarette in the office, to calm down.

Iris McMenzie

I left school in 1971 with 5 'O' levels and started working in Midland Bank. I remember that male colleagues weren't allowed to remove their jackets if they were working as cashiers and dealing with members of the public. We didn't have any computers and all bank statements were hand typed. If a customer's account went overdrawn their balance was typed in red – hence the saying 'in the red'.

Lynda Smoult

I started work with fifteen other lasses as a GPO telephonist in 1970. Our headsets had a trumpet-style mouthpiece, earphones and a plug at the end of a cord. Trainees' plugs had yellow tape around them so we were yellow banders. Red and green banders were qualified. I completed a month of training. For each call we connected a ticket like a lottery ticket had to be filled out, and we crossed off numbers in from and to fields. We needed to know all of the code numbers and codes for the towns. Time went slowly. We timed every call, looking at the clock constantly

I trained for faults position, emergency 999, clerical and directory enquiries. At 4ft 10ins, I stood on the bar beneath the swivel chair to reach the top of the switchboard. Supervisors stood behind us marching up and down the suites. Girls would hold their hands up, just like at school and ask a supervisor: 'Please Miss, can I slip out?'. It was called 'slipping out'. We weren't allowed to leave our position unless there was cover. Some workers were called the 'spares'. They ran around wearing their headsets at the ready. The 'spare' would plug in to your board to let you go. Never a minute was wasted. When we were really busy the supervisors would shout: 'Pick up another call!' We double booked, taking two at a time.

If anyone tried to make a personal call the supervisors were alerted, plugged a headset into a spare position and listened in. If anyone was caught, they were in real trouble.

It wasn't too strict though. If anyone wanted to be off early they would send a note up the positions: 'Please can anyone work from 5-6 for £1?' Anyone saving up to be married could make extra money from this and from working the odd hour to let someone away early. I took full advantage of this, sometimes working from 9am until 11pm.

There were rows of directories on enquiries. There were around six for London alone. We selected the appropriate book, looked through it for the number, not like the digital methods today. We timed calls and had to butt into conversations to ask for more money. At the time, telegrams were coming to the end of their life, things were changing.

In 1971 I was out on strike for six weeks, and we attended union meetings. Around forty lasses did go in and they were shouted at: 'Blacklegs, blacklegs!' I never lined up with the pickets. When we returned to work, some of these blacklegs left anyway as they were given the cold shoulder.

Later, I was sent to Longbenton Social Security Offices switchboard with four other lasses. At four o'clock I heard this deafening rumbling sound and felt tremors around my chair. I looked along to the others in alarm but none of them turned a hair: 'What's THAT?' 'Oh,' one of them said, 'It's just about 13,000 staff running for the buses.' It sounded like a herd of buffalos.

After repeating the same phrases hundreds of times a day, I once got on the bus and instead of asking for my fare, I said: 'Number please.'

Yvonne Young   *The GPO Telephone HQ photographed from Manors car park, 1971.*

After leaving school at eighteen my first job was for Dutton-Forshaw's, delivering spare parts to garages. There was a huge warehouse where you collected parts in a shopping trolley. I remember listening to The Three Degrees while doing that. I'd jump in the van and go all over Newcastle to tiny garages.

Then I joined Fenwick's as a trainee buyer, first in electricals, then in men's outfitting. There was a strict hierarchy about where the staff could eat. The merchants could eat in the public restaurant (we weren't allowed in there). There was the underbuyers' and buyers' lounge, and the hoi polloi ate in the staff restaurant. We had some good staff parties in the stockrooms. I joined the amateur dramatic society as it was a great way of meeting girls and the play we did was *Move Over Mrs Markham*. It involved me wearing body make-up for which I had to strip down to my Y-fronts! We performed in the theatre in Ellison Place, with Fenwick's props, and the men's clothes buyer was the director. Mohammed

Ali came to Fenwick's when he visited Newcastle in 1977, and choirs would come round at Christmas.

I got bored with that job after a while, and joined the family dry cleaning business.

Anon

In 1976, the Central Library introduced a cutting edge issue system. A lightpen read the book's barcode and entered it into a computer. In the 1970s we were allowed to wear trousers for work for the first time, but they had to be part of a trouser suit.

Kath Cassidy

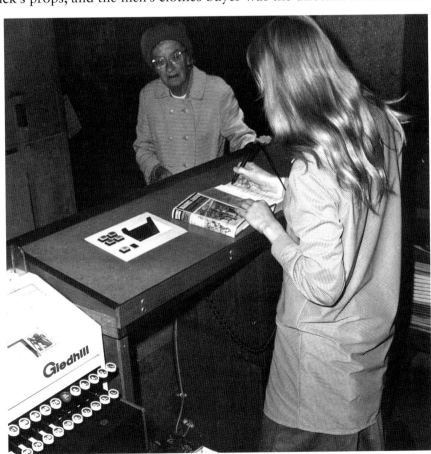

I worked for Hepworth the Tailors on Blackett Street. A lot of people from Norway came into Hepworth's. They were visiting Newcastle to buy our cheap goods. One day the manager was late opening up the shop and all the rest of the staff were waiting outside. When a foreign looking couple looked in the windows, Billy, who was one of our top salesmen and could sell snow to the Eskimos, went up to them and in pidgin English explained the shop would be open soon. He then asked them how far they had come. The reply was, 'Not far mate, Walker'.

Kevin Bell

Wherever you worked, you probably caught the bus. Marlborough Crescent bus station, 1975.

The coolest job

In 1975 I got the coolest Saturday job in the world at Windows in the Central Arcade.

I worked in the ground floor record department, selling everything from rock and disco to easy listening. The other Saturday girls and full time staff were good fun, on Saturdays the store was filled with beautiful young men (many had arrived on boats from Norway because shopping in England was so much cheaper for them), and, best of all, I got a generous staff discount so I was able to put together an enviable album collection at breakneck speed.

The worst thing was the pay. I got 30p an hour which added up to £2.40 a day. By the time I'd paid 2p National Insurance I took home £2.38. I envied my friend Karen who earned £4 a day in a tiny suburban flower shop, but if you'd asked me to swap I'd have been horrified.

In the 1970s album covers became works of art in their own right. They got fatter and fatter with inner and outer sleeves, gatefolds, moving parts and separate books of lyrics. This was all very well, unless you worked in a record shop and had to check every album for scratches before you sold it. All the unwrapping, unfolding, checking and putting back together again took ages. Pink Floyd's *Wish You Were Here* caused endless problems because the only way to get through the outer wrapping was to tear it. Pink Floyd fans looked on in horror as we mutilated this precious piece of artwork. Eventually the counter was supplied with razor blades so we could slit the outer covering without causing too much damage to the integrity of the album sleeve concept.

Vanessa Histon

Get a job, any job!

Having finally qualified (I didn't take to it naturally) in Electrical and Electronic Engineering I left Newcastle Polytechnic in 1971, at a time when there was no demand for my services. After spending some weeks scanning the *Chronicle* situations vacant columns for anything to do with what I had studied I got a prod from my girlfriend's father on the lines of 'Get a job, any job'. I'm not sure what the implied 'or else' was, but to keep things sweet I applied to be a porter at the new flagship Swallow Hotel above the Newgate Shopping Precinct. Its building in 1969 had followed that of two other prestige hotels in the 1960s, the Gosforth Park and the Five Bridges.

The wage was £16 a week plus a share of the tips. I learned how to clean the gents, polishing the porcelain with a fresh cloth ripped from the end of a roller towel; how to operate the switchboard, all cables and plugs with hundreds of holes to stick them in, while the telephonist went for her break; how to meet and greet guests, show them to their rooms and demonstrate the facilities such as the ultra modern headboard-mounted radio. If, say, a Japanese coach trip came in, the porters would leave the bags outside the rooms but I would make a point of knocking on all the doors not only to welcome guests but also to maximize my tips. Barry, the manager, was strict and maintained high standards at this high-class hotel which attracted many celebs including Pat Phoenix (Elsie Tanner) with husband and *Coronation Street* co-star Alan Browning, Chris Farlowe (I was a big fan), and the Manchester United team including Charlton, Law and Best, who scored the only goal that particular weekend. (Newcastle beat them 2-0 on the return visit to Manchester).

The controversial one-way system in the centre of Newcastle was introduced about this time and a number of very flustered drivers would arrive at reception through the pedestrian entrance on Newgate Street having driven in circles looking for the car park entrance on Fenkle Street. The simplest way to help was to accompany them and, on such an occasion, I climbed into a large black car to find the actor Wilfrid Hyde-White sitting in the back. He was charming as you might expect and reminisced about staying at the Turks Head in the old days. He gave me a £5 tip – a third of a week's wages!

Nic Grant

Students march past the Swallow Hotel on a dreary December day, 1971. This photo appeared in Courier.

Those super fans

ncjMedia

WE'LL SUPPORT YOU EVERMORE

HOWWAY THE LADS
NEWCASTLE UNITED
1973 · 1974

The Journal
Well done the lads!

May, 1974. The Journal welcomes manager Joe Harvey and the Newcastle United Football Team on their return from Wembley.

We went to St James's after the Wembley Cup Final to welcome the losers home. Only Newcastle would do that! My brother had made a black and white top hat to go to Wembley. (Margaret Taylor)

GOOD LUCK NEWCASTLE

NEWCASTLE

FROM **VG** the Convenient Store
AND THIER CUSTOMERS

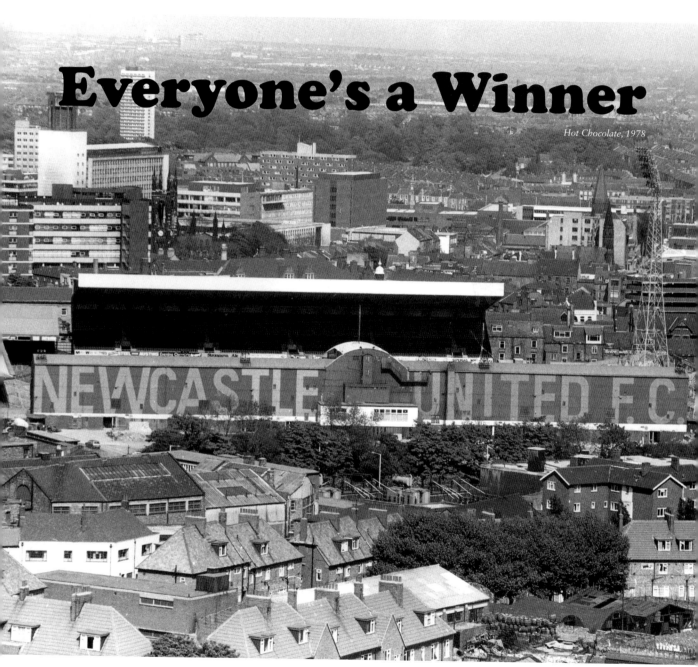

Everyone's a Winner

Hot Chocolate, 1978

St James's Park, 1975

The Magpies

A lot of my happiest memories of the 1970s involve Newcastle United. My first match was the 72/73 season against Ipswich, we lost 1-2 but I got to see my hero Supermac so I didn't mind. I remember the old Leazes End song, to the tune of the Christmas carol *Nowel, Nowel, Supermac, king of Newcastle.* We got our first colour TV that season, on the 23 September to be precise; it was a Murphy's and it came from Callers. Newcastle were playing Leeds and were actually on *Match of the Day* that night. We won 3–2 and it was great seeing it on our new TV – even the adverts looked good. I went to a game against Man United in the 73/74 season. George Best was playing but we still beat them 3–2 and two of the goals were by a local lad called George Hope who was playing instead of an injured Supermac.

Gary Robinson

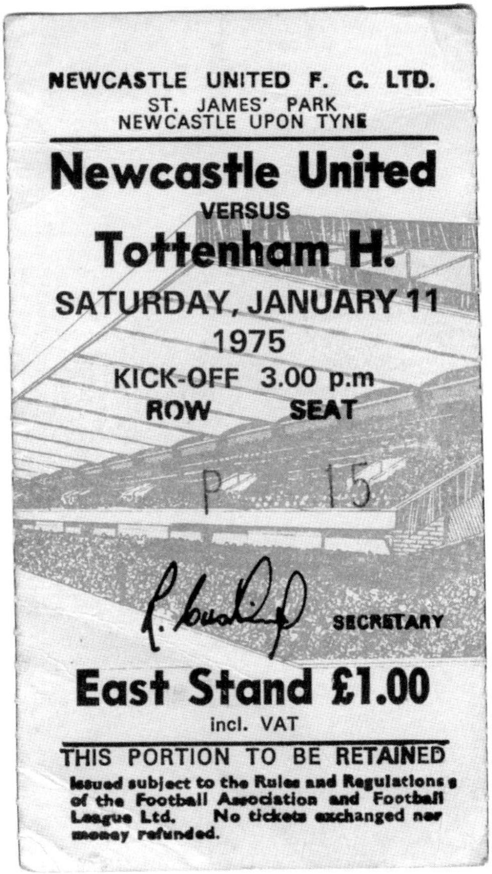
NEWCASTLE UNITED F. C. LTD.
ST. JAMES' PARK
NEWCASTLE UPON TYNE
Newcastle United
VERSUS
Tottenham H.
SATURDAY, JANUARY 11
1975
KICK-OFF 3.00 p.m
ROW SEAT
P 15
SECRETARY
East Stand £1.00
incl. VAT
THIS PORTION TO BE RETAINED
Issued subject to the Rules and Regulations of the Football Association and Football League Ltd. No tickets exchanged nor money refunded.

Gary Robinson

Gary Robinson's ticket for the Tottenham match, the first time he sat in the seats in the new East Stand.

An addiction

My first match was Newcastle v Tottenham and I was eight years old. It was the start of a football addiction. My dad and my uncle used to take me and my cousin, who was a year older. The man on the turnstile would put us both through together and pocket the rest of the ticket price. I'd be sat on the barrier, otherwise I wouldn't see anything. It was concrete and pebble-dashed … very painful on the legs after ninety minutes!

At one point we moved from the Gallowgate End to the Leazes End when they took the roof off. We wore knitted hats and scarves, and badges. No strips then.

Margaret Taylor

Off to Wembley

My brother and I were very excited about Newcastle going to Wembley in 1974 and wore our rosettes with pride. However – just like the following forty years – Newcastle lost 0-3 and were totally outplayed by Liverpool with a certain Kevin Keegan scoring twice. At least it prepared me for the future. Despite this early setback I have had a season ticket for the last twenty-five years!

Paul Donaghy

Paul (age seven) and Michael (age five) Donaghy, with their mother before the FA Cup Final, 1974.

In 1974 Newcastle United astonished everyone by reaching the FA Cup Final at Wembley for the first time since 1955.

As a journalist I churned out a stream of articles on Wembley-frenzied fans. There were the brothers whose mother knitted them black and white suits, and the supporter who spent a fortune on having his car professionally painted in black and white stripes with the club crest on the bonnet.

Travelling to London on a supporters' train, we sat opposite an elderly fan with, bizarrely, a small ventriloquist's dummy, dressed in black and white, on his knee. It continually said, in muffled fashion and to the point of utter tedium, 'Howay the lads'.

After the first of what was to be, over the next two decades, a traditional Wembley beating, the train left later that night for home. The same bloke was slumped comatose in his seat, the worse for strong drink, with the legs of the upturned dummy protruding from his large overcoat pocket. It summed up the day.

Tony Henderson

THE EMPIRE STADIUM, WEMBLEY

The Football Association Challenge Cup Competition

FINAL TIE

SAT., MAY 4, 1974
KICK-OFF 3 p.m.
YOU ARE ADVISED TO TAKE UP
YOUR POSITION BY 2.30 p.m.
1. This ticket is not transferable.
2. This counterfoil must be retained
for at least 6 months.

V.J.Litt CHAIRMAN'S
WEMBLEY STADIUM LTD

STANDING

TO BE RETAINED

£1.00

TURNSTILES
H
ENTRANCE
55
42 **WEST**
STANDING
ENCLOSURE

SEE PLAN AND CONDITIONS ON BACK

I thought beer was dear in the North East. A pint at my local in Barrow was 22½p yet we were paying 25p in Newcastle. As a marker I always use the ratio of the price to get in to see football to the price of a pint. So to watch Newcastle in 1976 was 75p (in the paddock – standing in those days) ratio 75/25 = 3. Nowadays you can pay £30 to watch the football (seated though) and £3 a pint, ratio 30/3 = 10. That's what you call inflation.

The highlight of my student days in Newcastle was going to Wembley to see Newcastle United in the League Cup Final in 1976. They were sadly beaten 2-1 by Manchester City and Denis Tuert's overhead kick. Me and my mate had a few pints in the Mens Bar in the Union then ran down to the bus station to catch the 10pm bus to London. We arrived something like 5:30am and kick off was not till 3pm. The return journey was the same 10pm till 5:30am. I remember when we got back we went to the Wimpey opposite the Civic Centre and both had the International Grill. When we finished we both looked at each other and said 'I could eat that again' so we did!

Roger Shaw

The best game ever was ...

Newcastle United v Nottingham Forest in the 1974 FA Cup at St James's Park. It had everything, 3 – 1 down, a riot when fans invaded the pitch, Pat Howard sent off, then Newcastle came back to win 4 – 3, with Bob Moncur scoring the winner. We all know what happened in the final but that's the Toon for you. Anyway my memories are of the Forest game and it was a fabulous day.

Mick Hamill

THE BLACK 'n' WHITE

NEWCASTLE UNITED versus

NOTTS FOREST

F.A. CUP 6TH ROUND

F.A. Cup 6th Rd. · Saturday, March 9th, 1974 · Kick-off 3.0 p.m.
Volume 2 No.25 · Official Match Day Magazine

10p

Toon Hero

I signed for Newcastle in May 1971 for the vast sum of £180,000. It was a Friday in London and Joe Harvey had come down for the Cup Final on the next day. I would have to have a medical to complete the transfer from Luton so I went up to Newcastle on the Monday. Luton's sponsor was George Twigg the car dealer so Luton's manager decided to send me up in style in a Rolls Royce. As we pulled up at St James's Park there was a gaggle of press waiting for me on the steps, and as I got out of the car a voice shouted 'This is the first time I've seen a player arriving in his signing on fee!' I passed the medical and sat in front of the press for questions. I did get the feeling some of them were not too happy about me joining Newcastle, they were ready to stick the knife in. After they'd finished, the crowd parted like the Red Sea as a figure walked through saying 'Welcome, you're going to love it here!' It was Jackie Milburn.

Later in the week Jackie drove me all round the area from Fenham to Blyth and Ashington. We talked about football as we drove, and what it meant to the North East, how it was a centre point. As we neared Ashington he pointed out a floodlit pitwheel and asked me 'Now Southerner... what's that?' Luckily I knew. He explained that 'On a Saturday the men who work under that pitwheel head to St James's Park. They'll be there by 2pm, and they'll welcome you onto the pitch. Now you have 90 minutes to make all their hard graft worthwhile. Every time you get the ball you have to make the most of it.' No pressure then! It was a big responsibility, that bond with the supporters.

My impression of Newcastle during those years was that it was a city waiting for something to happen. The value of the

Malcolm Macdonald, 23 January 1973.

riverside came to Newcastle a bit late to someone from London where I lived almost on the Thames. I used to go down to the quayside, and it was just a dead area of warehouses, waiting to be made beautiful. Newcastle was grimy and a little bit threatening, just like in *Get Carter*.

The football club never did anything properly it seemed. We used to train at Old Benwell Cricket Ground, and the pavilion was 1920s with no heating at all. Those 1970s winters were really cold so we'd get onto Joe Harvey, pointing out that he'd paid a lot for his players, surely he'd not want them coming down with pneumonia. Finally the message seemed to get through when a maintenance man arrived as we were about to get changed. They plugged a three-bar electric fire into the middle of the floor! We'd be discarding our soaking kit onto the floor, going into the bath and coming out even wetter. Sheer madness!

When I left for Arsenal in 1976 I did miss how easy it was to get to St James's Park from Morpeth where I lived. I missed the

Bobby in Dominant Mood
A fine leap by Bobby Moncur against Liverpool

Mick Hamill (from NUFC 1974 Notts Forest programme)

fans too of course, and their fantastic support, but I always felt with Newcastle, whoever's in charge, they take their fans for granted.

The moment I'll treasure from my time at Newcastle has to be my first 1971 home match of the season against Liverpool on August 21. I'll never forget it. I hadn't scored in the two previous away games. The day had been a bit different from the start as that morning we went to a local bookshop to sign Bobby Moncur's new book which had just come out. After lunch off we went to St James's Park and onto the field at five to three. After I had scored from a penalty and equalised to 1-1 I got another good ball and scored again. There was a hushed silence, and I think the crowd knew they'd got someone who could surprise them. Later in the second half I got another good left foot goal into the far corner of the net, and the ice was broken from then on. The thing that made it even more special came after that second goal, and the silence followed by a roar, and then the crowd of nearly 40,000 began to sing to the tune of *Jesus Christ Super Star* only the words were 'Supermac, Superstar, how many goals have you scored so far?' How did they do it? How did they all sing this together? I'll never forget it.

Malcolm Macdonald

The rebel shareholder

When my father died in 1973 I inherited his shares in Newcastle United, I had always been a fervent follower. Fenton Braithwaite, a director, suggested I too should become a director. For the next five years I became, in the words of the *Evening Chronicle*'s John Gibson, the rebel shareholder. I didn't become a director but managed to protect the interests of the other shareholders and the supporters with a succession of extraordinary meetings and even a High Court action.

I was instrumental in forming the NSA (Newcastle Supporters Association) in 1977. We bought a prime site in Gallowgate and built the Gallowgate Club. We even had our own newspaper, *The Supporter*, a forerunner of the modern day fanzine. We sold enough adverts to pay for 20,000 copies per edition.

The team never really succeeded but gave a lot of pleasure to us fans. We got to the FA Cup Final in 1974 and the League Cup final in 1976, but lost both. Malcolm Macdonald was the hero.

Malcolm Dix

Malcolm Dix tries to gain a seat on the Newcastle United Board, December, 1976.

ncjMedia

Float like a butterfly, sting like a bee: Muhammad Ali's visit to Tyneside

Muhammad Ali arrived on Tyneside through the efforts of painter and decorator Johnny Walker, who had the dream of going to America and inviting Ali to come to Tyneside to help raise funds for boys' clubs on Tyneside. He was sponsored by two local business men to fly to Chicago to somehow convince Ali to come to Newcastle for no fee. Amazingly, he succeeded.

On 14 July 1977 Ali arrived with his family and a few days later even had his recent marriage to Veronica Porche blessed at a South Shields Mosque. I met him at the Grainger Park boxing club on 15 July and got a formal invitation to meet him at the Lord Mayor's Mansion House that evening.

Ali was filmed at Eldon Square for a national broadcast when he said Newcastle was 'nicer than America' and at one point was pinned against an escalator by enthusiastic women and children!

The Friendship Force was the brainchild of an American, Wayne Smith, who worked with President Carter to foster friendship between nations. He organised 250 citizens from Georgia, USA, to visit Newcastle in July 1977, which coincided with Muhammad Ali's visit. Wayne managed to persuade Ali to address a dinner for the Friendship Force at the Civic Centre.

Russell Routledge

Muhammad Ali at the Grainger Park Boys Club, 15 July, 1977. Ali was sparring with a local eighteen-year-old, Les Close.

And a different ball game ...

Gosforth's 1st XV were emerging as the top rugby union team in the North East in the early 1970s. They would go on to win the John Player Cup in 1976 and 1977 and become the best team in England with a lot of Internationals playing for them – Roger Uttley, Peter Dixon, Malcolm Young, Duncan Madsen, Richard Breakey and Brian Patrick to name but a few.

Malcolm Dix

Above, John Bull Repair Kit perform on the empty space at the top of Blackett Street, 22 September 1971, as part of the Newcastle Festival. What was that all about?

Right, Bernard Brasseur, fire eater, entertains the crowds on Clayton Street, June 1978. (ncjMedia)

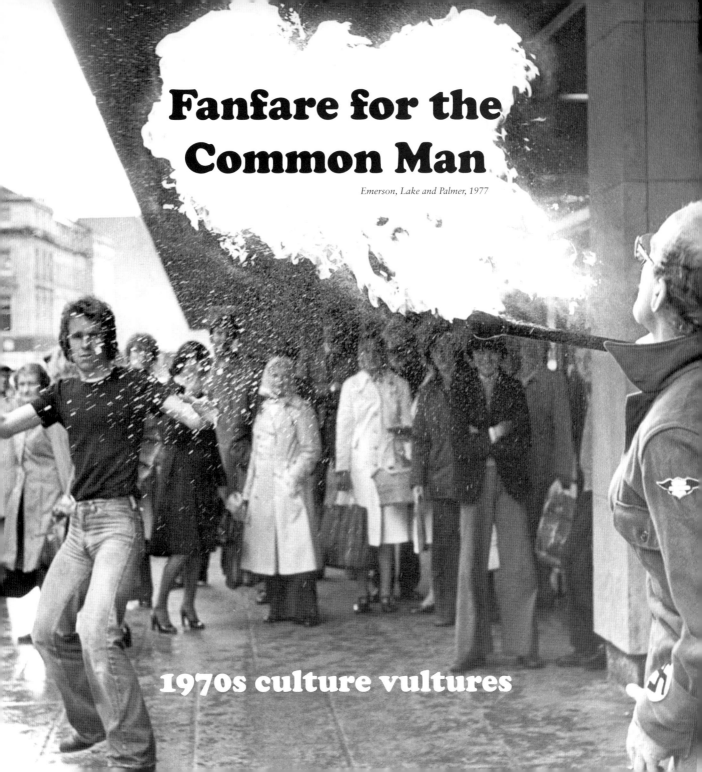

Fanfare for the Common Man

Emerson, Lake and Palmer, 1977

1970s culture vultures

Newcastle's festival for the people

Newcastle Festival kicked off over two weeks in Autumn 1969 with a budget of £50,000. In 1970 it was accused of 'pseudo culture' but held seventy flamboyant events with an open air talent contest in Eldon Square. By 1971 the festival was under control of the Council's Arts Working Group and a Festival Trust. In 1972 it was accused of snobbery, but was well attended. The 1973 line-up included Andy Warhol films at the Tyneside Film Theatre, 'filmgoers walked out in disgust' (*The Journal*), Derek Jacobi at the Theatre Royal, classical concerts, Cézanne at the Laing, ballet, and comedy. In 1974 with an increased budget it was judged 'dull and irrelevant'.

Newcastle Festival publicity on the Haymarket, 1970.

In 1975 entrepreneur Andy Hudson was appointed to make the festival more local and more fun and timing was changed to June. Central events would combine with ten community festivals. There were jazz and blues concerts, *Carry On* films, drama, and Northern Sinfonia put on a baroque concert at the City Hall to recreate the atmosphere of St Mark's Venice! Late drinking to 11.30pm was allowed in the City Tavern, Royal Archer and Farmer's Rest. 1976 was a big success too.

In 1977 there were more money problems and low audiences but the Tyneside Cinema was popular, as was the Bedrock Festival at the University Theatre. Electronic sculptures at the Laing were popular, and Billy Connolly went down a storm.

A shorter 1978 bash included food, film, and literary events including, from America, William Burroughs. In 1979 the line-up included Tennessee Williams, Larry Grayson, Roy Castle, Quentin Crisp, poet Allen Ginsberg, Mary Whitehouse, and Pan's People.

Anna Flowers

Most of all I remember the Newcastle Festival in 1976 because I was on a clerical traineeship scheme with the city council and attached to the festival office. We had lots of great artists including Larry Adler, George Melly, and Last Exit. I remember Sting in his stripy top. There was a Hoffnung exhibition in the Civic Centre basement which Frances Tomelty, Sting's then wife, curated. There was a street parade to open the festival.

Carol Rocke

Classical Concerts
Lunchtimes and
Late Nights

City Hall Concerts

Poetry
Exhibitions

Films
Theatre

Folk
Jazz
and Pop

Talks Lectures
Outdoor Events
Other Events

Newcastle Festival

17th June-3rd July 1977

Above, Pan's People performed at a Festival Variety Extravaganza at the University Theatre in June 1979. Top, Jesmond Festival fun, 1977.

God Save the Queen

While I was a student, living on Wingrove Avenue, we decided to have a street party for the Queen's Jubilee. Everyone brought some food and drink and we put bunting up. My Mum was up visiting from London and she was very impressed at the community spirit. Lots of people were unemployed but they were amazingly stoic and cheerful. (I bet they thought we were posh twits but they were always friendly and helpful.) As soon as we were ready to start the skies opened so some of the men 'accessed' an empty house and we had the party in there. That was typical of Newcastle folk – very resourceful.

Patricia Fenton (née Glaves) (Ncle 1973-78)

I gave birth to both my children in The Princess Mary Maternity Hospital. My first child, a son, was born in 1977, the Queen's Silver Jubilee year. I remember carrying my baby son in my arms in his hand-knitted matinee coat and rompers to see the royal couple when they visited Newcastle as part of their celebration tour. A fantastic memory – a sea of union jacks.

Lynda Smoult

Crowds on Gosforth High Street celebrate the Queen's visit, 15 July 1977.

The Gosforth Hotel was the venue for many Last Exit gigs, and, in 1979, for the birth of the Donald brothers' Viz Comic.

15 July, 1977, and the crowds in Eldon Square turn out for the Queen's Silver Jubilee visit to Newcastle.

Live, and other theatrical experiences

I had been politicised by the Miners' strike of 1972 and was living in Exeter, when I saw an advert in *The Guardian* for what I felt would be a 'proper' job, helping to run a new venture called Live Theatre in Newcastle. It wasn't paid work; you signed on the Dole and got around £2 a week, and if you got some paid work you signed off, then on again. We put on short plays in working men's clubs, and I had to sell these clubs the idea of letting us use a room for free performances. There was no office, just me in a phone box and going round the clubs. Women weren't allowed in the bars then, so I'd be sent to wait in the concert room before trying to convince them they wanted a performance. We wanted to get away from the idea of traditional theatre and felt part of a political ferment. We were linked with the Workers Revolutionary Party. It shows how paranoid we were in those days when I took £20 and put it in a drawer in case the banks collapsed. Live Theatre joined forces with the Amber Collective and eventually got premises to work from. In a sense you had to sell out to become successful. There was a bit of a divide in Live Theatre between the people who had been to university, or were teachers, and the actors who were working class. The whole point was that this was new talent from people who otherwise would not have had a voice. Eventually Live Theatre launched the careers of actors and writers like Jimmy Nail, Tim Healy, Kevin Whately, Robson Greene and Lee Hall.

Geraldine McClelland

The University Theatre

I became the photographer at the University Theatre in 1973. I saw many fine productions including an early production of *Close the Coal House Door* and a few that were less than brilliant, including the lamentable *Orgy*. In the cast was a red setter and one night I heard an audience member saying 'well, the dog was very good'!

Rik Walton

Michael Atwell performs in Orgy.

The University Theatre along with the more experimental Gulbenkian Studio, established itself from 1971 as the place to be seen. We saw Peter Shaffer's wonderful *Equus* there in 1975. The theatre bar was the scene for live music, in winter it was a good place to share a drink and a conversation with like-minded students and free-thinkers, in summer we could often be found on the steps fronting the car park that looked across to the Civic Centre. I remember intense discussions about politics, exhibitions and music. It was a strange time!

The American cult writer William Burroughs appeared as part of the Newcastle Literary Festival in June 1978. His reading at the University's Curtis Auditorium was very well attended. I particularly remember Joe Strummer and Paul Simonon of The Clash sitting in the row in front. Burroughs, wearing a shiny blue suit and matching trilby and carrying a briefcase, looked like an insurance salesman. He gave a fine reading of short excerpts from his books, including the *Naked Lunch*. The following evening he gave a reading at the Morden tower.

Anthony Flowers

Hair... the shock of the nude

Hair, the 'tribal love-rock musical' opened at the Theatre Royal on 28 October 1970 to an audience with an average age of 21. It famously featured a short scene where the cast appeared starkers. That's not why we went, the music was great.

Anna Flowers

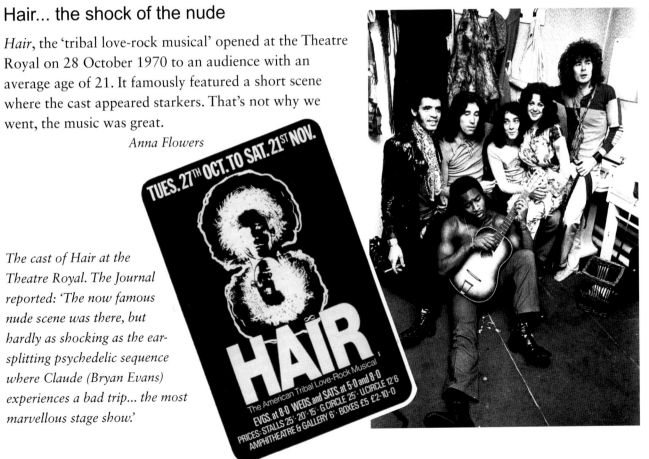

ncjMedia

The cast of Hair at the Theatre Royal. The Journal reported: 'The now famous nude scene was there, but hardly as shocking as the ear-splitting psychedelic sequence where Claude (Bryan Evans) experiences a bad trip... the most marvellous stage show.'

Oh Babe What Would You Say?

We started going to Morden Tower readings in 1968 while it was still in its heyday and poetry in general was the new rock'n'roll.

It was not a salubrious venue, down a dark lane, with no street lighting. The Tower had no heating, precious little seating and no facilities, but it hosted readings by a wide and varied number of poets, both British and American. In those early days, each reading was packed, with people sitting crammed together on the floor or jammed onto the windowsills. Everyone met at the Northumberland Arms, on the corner of Stowell Street and it was there that the female members of the audience went to use the Ladies. The blokes were less inhibited and part of the dankness of that dark lane was down to them.

David James

Ric Caddel reads at Morden Tower, Connie Pickard (founder, with Tom Pickard, of the Morden Tower Bookroom) left, Gael Turnbull right, 14 February 1975.

By 1974, Tom and Connie Pickard had split up. Tom moved away and Connie ran the Morden Tower readings with the help of volunteers, including Ric. Though the poets who came to read were still from a wide and avant-garde field, the audience was smaller and less enthusiastic than the early days and it was never quite the same.

Ann Caddel

Ultima Thule grew out of the Morden Tower Bookroom, and moved from No. 16 into 22 Handyside Arcade in the early 1970s. Poet Tony Jackson, the spitting image of American Beat poet Allen Ginsberg, a partner in the bookshop with poets Tom

ULTIMA THULE bookshop

QUITE SIMPLY THE MOST ADVENTUROUS BOOKSHOP ANYWHERE IN THE AREA.

POETRY - FICTION
DRAMA - FILMSCRIPTS
SMALL PRESS PUBLICATIONS
EASTERN RELIGIONS -
2nd HAND RECORDS -
ALL THE UNDERGROUND PRESS.

22 Arcadia, Percy Street, Newcastle.
Tel. 23679.

Pickard and Jon Silkin, was often to be found in charge. From behind the counter, Tony would closely observe his potential customers, sceptical that they would actually make a purchase, and ever watchful for shoplifters. He was assisted at weekends by a young aspiring writer, Brian Marley. Ultima Thule finally closed in late 1974.

Anthony Flowers

Ultima Thule on Handyside Arcade opposite Kard Bar was the ultimate hippy shop, beads, bangles, strange looking pipes and long cigarette papers. Everything the average 'head' could want.

Chris Mabbott

David James photographed many of the Morden Tower readings and took this shot of Ultima Thule's shop front in the early 1970s.

A decade forged in Iron

I drove out of the Sixties in my battered old Landrover in September 1970, and fetched up on Tyneside. Everything I owned was in the back of that vehicle; I was a brash freewheeling young journalist, who'd worked two years on a London weekly newspaper (*Walthamstow Guardian*). The next career move was a stint on a regional morning, *Newcastle Journal*, after which (or so the plan went) I'd return South, storm Fleet Street, and become the next Bernard Levin.

I vividly remember that first day, stopping the Landrover on the Tyne Bridge to ask two gadgies in flat caps the directions to the Jesmond B & B guest house. The gadgies explained the route. I listened, nodded, thanked them and drove off. I hadn't understood a single word they'd said. What kind of outpost had I come to? Where was the interpreter?

Priorities change. I slowly realised I was more in love with the North East than in becoming a Fleet Street hack. In my student days, as others enjoyed the Sixties excesses, I'd been short-haired and fairly non-indulgent. Now as my contemporaries put on suits and forged careers with Barclays Bank, I became hirsute, and donned hippy gear. I'd always been a slow developer.

I did need to write for a living, but slaving forty hours a week for a newspaper mogul was not the right formula. A landmark was the founding of the magazine IRON in 1973. I was living at the time with poet Tom Pickard and his wife Connie in Gateshead, helping them run Morden Tower, mixing with other poets and artists. What more logical step than to set up set my own litmag?

At the start there was simply the magazine. Individual IRON Press books began two years later. I spent my entire savings of £300 on an electronic typewriter and bashed out every single word of edition number one myself – any mistakes had to be retyped and the single line cut out and pasted in using cow gum, an adhesive said, after long exposure, to have hallucinatory effects ...

All titles and headlines were hand-done with Letraset – each letter pressed down onto the page from a plastic sheet. I cadged help and advice from the lay-out men at *The Journal*, and in the quiet small hours we'd paste up the pages in the newsroom. At my own expense, I printed 500 copies of edition one, which included in its twenty-eight pages, fifteen writers. I gave almost all of them away.

All this so impressed Northern Arts, they offered me a grant for edition two, and slowly IRON established itself as part of the vibrant small-mag scene in the region.

Peter Mortimer

Strong Words

Inspired by writer Jack Common, Dr Keith Armstrong established, with others, Tyneside Poets in 1973 and the Strong Words community publishing project in 1977. Its aim was to publish booklets based on the lives and experiences of working people in the area, expressed through the words of the people themselves.

Along with the likes of Common, I had a sense of the industrial heritage of Newcastle, and a sense of community. With this in mind, from the early 1970s I worked as a community development worker, poet, librarian and publisher and organised community arts festivals in the West End and Byker and many literary events featuring the likes of Yevgeny Yevtushenko, Douglas Dunn, Barry Hines, Edward Bond, Edwin Morgan, Jon Silkin and Ivor Cutler ... We felt we could change things in those distant seventies – and we did, in a small yet beautiful way.

Keith Armstrong

Keith Armstrong

MICHAEL WILKIN, Gordon Phillips, Peter Mortimer, Alan Brown and Keith Armstrong are all members of The Tyneside Poets.

Painter Man

A warm Friday in June 1970 marked my last day at Newcastle College of Art. That evening at the Burton House with my bricklayer friend Ernie Usher, I explored the problems of my artistic goals versus financial survival. Ernie needed a labourer and recruited me with the job description, 'wor lass could dee it!'. I would keep fit, get a tan and earn money as a hod carrier. Thanks to Ernie and a succession of other people who employed me for the next eight years, I continued my art, and earned a living.

ncjMedia

Richard Flynn at the Laing Art Gallery in September 1979 with the view of All Saints painted during the freezing winter of 1978-1979.

My principal subject then was the Grainger Market, a packed, booming place where the barrow boys constantly rolled past with the cry 'mind ya legs'. When the balcony café went out of business I used the space as a base that became a studio. Here I could record the bustle below.

I soon expanded my subject matter to the rest of Tyneside and the Northumberland coast, and by 1975 I was more confident that I could make a living from painting, but as winter approached I retreated to my base in the Grainger Market then returned to the construction industry, working for William Leech on a large housing estate project in Jarrow. I began to sketch my fellow workers during breaks, giving each drawing to the sitter and soon realised the importance William Leech placed on a good public image and philanthropy. Eventually I proposed an artist in residence idea and, amazingly, the company accepted my proposal.

Leech's public relations consultant, Jack Ramsey, got to work with the media. One week earlier I had been down a manhole! 'Saved! A talent from going down the drain' was the heading in the *Daily Mail*.

I was given a studio in the Leech offices on City Road, just in time for one of the most frigid winters on record. The window overlooked All Saints and I began an oil painting of the church, together with several pastels exploring the atmospheric light over the Tyne. In early 1979 Jack Ramsey successfully proposed an exhibition to the Laing Art Gallery. He also organised a reception for my work at the Mansion House when my painting of All Saints was presented to the Lord Mayor, Peggy Murray.

That summer of 1979 a major exhibition of Impressionist masters had opened in the newly renovated Laing only to immediately close after the theft of two small works. After a year of hard work, in late September my own exhibition of 56 works was screwed securely to the wall. Six-hundred people attended the opening, including old Grainger Market friends. It was the opening I had dreamed about, I just managed to get through my speech!

The previous days had been overshadowed by the news of Lord Mountbatten's assassination in Mullaghmore but in a hectic week when ITV was on strike, an overworked BBC team turned up the day before the show and their film was shown on *Look North*. With one TV channel, it meant most of the population of the North of England watched the show. The momentum of success continued, fifty of the fifty-six works were sold. The exhibition had broken all attendance and sales records!

Richard Flynn

April 1978 saw the opening of a ground-breaking exhibition at the Laing Gallery, which then went on tour to galleries and museums throughout the UK for the next two years. The exhibition, '100 Years of Enamel Signs', featured the joint collection of Andrew Morley and Christopher Baglee, graduates of Newcastle University in Fine Art and Architecture, as well as signs loaned by a few other collectors of enamel advertising signs from around the country. The accompanying book soon sold out.

Christopher Baglee

Sometimes we'd go to Spectro Arts centre in Bells Close and the Robert Self Gallery on High Bridge, Live Theatre and late night films at the Tyneside Cinema. Performance Art was then the emerging art form, leaving a lot of us a bit bewildered!

Vera Faulkner

Andrew Morley and Christopher Baglee Archive

Get Carter!

It was 1970 and I was waiting to start a new job, but had a fortnight to spare, when my wife spotted an advert in the *Evening Chronicle* to be an extra in a film being made on Tyneside. I thought I'd give it a go. The interviews were in a run down old warehouse where the Copthorne is now and there were hundreds of people all waiting to be extras. When I got to the end of the queue I was surprised when the guy there asked it I'd like to do stand-in work for one of the stars, John Osborne. I'd just have to sit there while they got the lighting and the cameras right and then the star would come in and do his bit of acting. Fine with me!

We got picked up at the Station hotel, where most of the stars were staying, and were driven by taxi to a massive house in County Durham, called The Heights in the film. There was CCTV on the gates and fancy cars in the cellars. I didn't see much of John Osborne, he seemed quite a dour person.

And that's what I did for the fortnight I was working on *Get Carter*. Some of the takes took ages, and there was a lot of heavy drinking going on back

Michael Caine at the Central Station, August 1970.

then with some of the stars, but Michael Caine was a very pleasant man. He said he found the landscape up here a bit rugged and preferred the rolling hills of the south!

There was a lot of violence up here then, especially in the west end, a gangland kind of culture, so the film reflected that.

I couldn't go to the end of filming party unfortunately as I had to start that new job. Mind you the money for working on *Get Carter* was £8 a day, which was really good money back then. I went to see the film when it came to North Shields the following year.

Chris Dawson

This rare view (from a scratched negative) of the interior of the Haymarket Cinema was taken in December 1971 at a student rally. (Dr Jekyll and Sister Hyde was showing that week.)

In March 1971 Get Carter opened in Newcastle at the ABC Haymarket. It was gritty, violent ... and it was all about our city! We recognised the places, were confused by how the stars emerged from the city centre and were immediately miles away, but Newcastle, a grimy, quite scary place in the early 1970s, was clearly as much of a star as Michael Caine.

The Tyneside Cinema was in its heyday in the 1970s and often showed obscure films, which, for some reason I was drawn to but never seemed to enjoy. But I still felt the need to support it probably due to its size, and cult status and the fact it was so unique, forever in the shadow of the Odeon across the road.

Simon Carey

We saw some memorable non-mainstream films at the Tyneside Film Theatre, from Herzog to Pasolini. It was a treat on many Friday nights after an unpleasant week of teaching practice. But I didn't altogether enjoy the Andy Warhol festival season in 1973... I would have walked out of the three-hour long and incredibly boring *Chelsea Girls*, but didn't want to look uncool.

Anna Flowers

It was in the 1970s when I first cultivated a love for the cinema. At that time, despite a number of screen closures, Newcastle still had several cinemas, the flagship being the Odeon in Pilgrim Street. In the early 1970s, like so many large cinemas, it was converted into a multi-screen auditorium by turning the old ground-floor stalls

The Tyneside Film Theatre, 1971. It closed in 1975 but reopened in 1976 as the Tyneside Cinema.

into Odeons 2 and 3, leaving the upper Circle as Odeon 1 (later a further screen, Odeon 4, was added).

Despite these changes, Odeon 1, with its plush velvet seating and rich décor, was still an exciting place to watch a film and the big screen was ideally suited to blockbusters. Films I remember seeing there include *The Spy Who Loved Me*, *The Wild Geese*, *Close Encounters of the Third Kind* and (right at the start of the decade), *The Aristocats*. Of course, a hot dog and Kia-Ora were also part of the film experience!

Just up the road, tucked away in a narrow alley off Northumberland Street, leading to the Central Library, was the Queen's, another cinema with just a single screen, where I saw *Carry On Behind*, *Royal Flash* and (the final film I saw there), *Zulu Dawn*. The Queen's, like the Odeon, was owned by the Rank Organisation and films that started at the Queen's often moved onto one of the smaller Odeon screens before ending their run. The two cinemas were barely a hundred yards apart and so it probably made commercial sense for Rank to close the Queen's in the late 1970s and sell the site – nevertheless, it was a fine cinema and a sad loss.

At the top of the Haymarket was the ABC, another traditional single-screen auditorium, where I saw *Murder on the Orient Express* with my parents, and the Frank Langella-Laurence Olivier version of *Dracula* in 1978. Despite its fine location, EMI (who owned the ABC chain) seemed to downgrade it as the decade wore on, moving most of their big releases (like *Death on the Nile*) to their other city centre auditorium, the two-screen ABC Westgate Road. The poor old Haymarket was starved of investment and, instead of blockbusters, typical fare on offer included low-budget horror films or cheaply produced imports that had no stars to speak of, but were released on a region-by-region basis accompanied by saturation TV coverage.

The Westgate Road cinema was a nice enough place to watch a film but suffered from its location, on the edge of the city centre, in an area that had seen better days. Nearby was the giant Stoll cinema that had once screened big releases like *Where Eagles Dare*, but now survived on a seedy diet of 'adult' films prior to its reincarnation and restoration as the Tyne Theatre.

John Bourne

There was a bit of a scam going on at the ABC Haymarket where a couple of lads would buy tickets for a film and then one of them would open the fire exit door to let the rest in! At this time you could go into a film at anytime (not just at the beginning, and stay in all day if you liked). Another time at the Haymarket it was all quiet during the film and then someone started screaming their head off – there was a mouse running up her leg!

Irene Soulsby

We queued for hours to see Star Wars at the Odeon in 1977, the line went right round the corner. I was just a little kid, but the experience of seeing that film was unforgettable. However, I was taken to the toilet about a third way through, so for years I had no idea what motivated Luke to leave Tattooine!

Kemi Kilburn

The view from the new Central Library, July 1970. Hello Dolly is playing at the Queen's Cinema.

On the telly

In 1974 I joined Tyne Tees Television where I would stay for the next eighteen years. Back then it produced an amazing variety of regional and some network programming with departments for Arts, Current Affairs, News, Sport, Farming, Religion, Drama, Light Entertainment and so on. It employed around 500 staff and its loss has been a sad one. To illustrate how some attitudes have changed, if we had a bit of a heat wave a crew would be briefed to get shots of 'tottie' on Tynemouth long sands to brighten up *Today at Six* and we even had a 'Miss Wet T-shirt' competition one year!

Nic Grant

Tyne Tees Television studios, City Road, 1977. Egypt Cottage, next door, was a regular for the staff.

Lyn's Look-In

I was teaching at Heworth Grange School in 1975 when I saw an advert in the *Evening Chronicle* for a Tyne Tees continuity announcer. It was a big deal in those days when there was only BBC1, BBC2 and ITV. My continuity pieces grew into much more and eventually the Union said 'that's not continuity, that's a programme', so we ran a competition for a title for a new children's show and *Lyn's Look-In* won. My co-presenter was Malcolm Gerrie. We had a talking parrot and a squelchy snake called Sisilly, which the kids could sit on. It was really popular.

I left in 1979 to have my first child, but came back after only six weeks to co-present *Check it Out*, a show for teenagers. That year, wearing a ghastly yellow dress, I sat in on an interview with Johnny Rotten and his band Public Image Limited, and presenter Chris Cowie, which was a difficult experience – Johnny caused the expected mayhem! You can still see it on U Tube. That same show we interviewed Sting, who I knew from college. He wasn't too pleased when I called him Gordon.

In the studios at Tyne Tees Television. Lyn was voted 'the sexiest bird on television' by Sunday Sun readers in January 1976.

When I was a student doing teacher training I had long hair, wore jeans, a hippie look. At Tyne Tees we'd wear jeans for under the desk but you needed colourful tops. I had a great yellow top with polka dots which I'd wear with a blue jacket. I had twenty-eight jackets! (Lyn Spencer)

I used to buy clothes from Fenwick's, Bainbridge's, C & A, Leaf and of course Marcus Price. I bought my wedding dress at Richards Shops for around £12, but my hat was £26 from Fenwick's French Salon. That was a lot of money! When I was teaching in 1975 I earned about £1,800, and when I got the Tyne Tees job I never asked what the pay was because I wanted the job so much. When my contract arrived and the salary was £3,600, I couldn't believe it! That was more money than a lot of men earned. I just spent it. I loved Enny handbags from Fenwick's. I think I spent about £80 on one, and my father said 'How much?'.

It was sink or swim at Tyne Tees but I met some fab people. I think I got on because I was very friendly girl-next-door type of person, not too glam. There was a big staff, someone to do everything. You couldn't move a chair or get a glass of water yourself because the Unions had someone for that job. There was a lot of money around, taxis everywhere, and an allowance for clothes.

Lyn Spencer

In December 1978 our class from Dumpling Hall Middle School was chosen to appear on the Saturday morning programme *Lyn's Look-In* on Tyne Tees. We recorded the programme on a Thursday and had the whole day off school. We met at the school and were taken to the studio and given T-shirts to wear for the show. We were shown around the studio and met Lyn and Malcolm who introduced the show. The show was a mixture of music and making things. Rod Stewart's *Do Ya Think I'm Sexy* was Number 1. When the show was being recorded I and two of my classmates had to sit and model tea cosies on our heads, to show children how to make an interesting present for your Mam or your Grandma for Christmas! After the show was finished we were taken to the green room where a buffet had been laid on for us.

Cheryl Howitt

The 1970s was a decade in which a whole generation were able to aspire to what many of their parents could not – home ownership and the other trappings of shading from working to middle class such as a car and white collar jobs. The hit BBC TV series *Whatever Happened to the Likely Lads?*, set in Newcastle, perfectly caught the inherent tensions and comic content of this period of transition. The series was broadcast between 1973-1974 as the colour sequel to the mid-1960s hit *The Likely Lads*. Terry Collier, played by James Bolam, represents the traditional Geordie male. His best mate Bob Ferris (Rodney Bewes) is in the painful process of making the middle-class move to the Elm Lodge private housing estate with his primly aspirational wife Thelma. Bob is torn between the local bar and the requirement to attend Thelma's fondue parties, much to Terry's sardonic amusement.

Tony Henderson

Radio Star: BBC Radio Newcastle 1970-79

It is early in the morning of January 7, 1971. I am sitting behind a microphone in a radio studio on the second floor of a remarkably unattractive 1960s office block in Archbold Terrace, Jesmond.

At precisely ten seconds to 7am, my colleague at the control desk flicks a switch and my headphones crackle to life. A brief electronic jingle tells our listeners that this is BBC Radio Newcastle broadcasting on 95.4VHF. 'Good morning. It is seven o'clock and we welcome you to the first day of the new radio station serving Newcastle and Tyneside. Now the news read by Dick Godfrey.'

I had been in the North-East for a little over two years, initially earning my living as a journalist on *The Journal*. When the BBC started recruiting for a new local radio station, I got a job as a reporter/producer/presenter. My job gave me a close view of the developments the decade had in store. For example, the first day of tunnelling for the Metro saw me on top of Grey's Monument at first light to report on traffic problems expected because of road closures.

I interviewed T. Dan Smith on his release from prison where he had served a sentence for corruption. I was at Wallsend for the launch of the super tanker *Esso Northumbria* designed to bring oil around the Cape to avoid the Middle East. I was at the Civic Centre when visiting US President Jimmy Carter greeted the welcoming crowd with 'Howay the lads!'

As the decade progressed, I expanded my radio role. How about putting ordinary people on the air to talk about whatever concerned them? It appeared outrageous and risky, but that was the nature of the times. In May, 1974, the daily programme I called *Hotline* went on the air. I don't claim to have invented the phone-in, but I believe that mine was one of the first in the UK.

Soon competition loomed when the new commercial station, Metro, appeared. Its phone-in was late night and presented by James Whale, whose audience liked to sneak outrageous language past him. My daytime audience were more respectful. They called me Mr Godfrey.

It was an exciting experience. I appeared to be tapped into the concerns and interests of the nation. My most vivid memory is of the morning after the Birmingham pub bombings by the IRA. I had a sense that people were on the

Dick Godfrey, radio star, late 1970s.

BEDROCK

Simply the best rock show around.

verge of erupting with anti-Irish sentiment and even action. It was not my place to put a cap on the volcano, but I think allowing some people to let off steam in public helped.

My main interest was in music. I grew my hair long, expanded the width of my flares and sported an ear-ring. I started a late night rock show called – quite cleverly, I felt – *Bedrock* and recruited a team of volunteer reviewers and interviewers from the enthusiastic fans in my audience.

Musicians turned up on Monday evenings with demo tapes. We played their music and talked of their ambitions. Among them was a singer/bass player in a jazz-rock band called Last Exit. His name was Gordon, but he preferred to be known as Sting.

My *Bedrock* team formed a rock co-operative with the musicians and set about opening new venues wherever we could, mostly in pubs. The Northumberland Arms on the Quayside was a favourite venue along with the Cooperage further along and the Bridge Hotel which already had a thriving folk scene led by the High Level Ranters.

But the best gig wasn't one of ours, although we did occasionally manage to get some of our bands on the bill as supporting acts. Friday nights at the Mayfair were weekly services for devotees. Top national and international bands played there and the best of our local bands were eager to take to the same stage.

Some certainly appeared to have futures. Geordie, for example, had a spirited lead singer called Brian Johnson. The band made a couple of albums, but Johnson left to join a bunch called AC/DC.

And, of course, there was the most noted of our bands, Lindisfarne, with Alan Hull as front-man. The band rejected pop stardom in favour of life in Newcastle where they became what drummer Ray Laidlaw memorably described to me as 'the town band'.

Bedrock begat an annual rock festival as part of the broader Newcastle Festival which had started in the late 1960s. The first was in Newcastle Polytechnic, but the Guildhall on the Quayside was the venue for subsequent Bedrock Festivals.

The last Bedrock Festival ended the decade in 1979. A new form of music had surfaced in the form of punk rock. The leading local exponents were the Angelic Upstarts from South Shields. The climax of their set was an anti-police song which involved tossing a pig's head into the audience. At the Guildhall, they were a shade too enthusiastic and a girl in the front row was knocked out.

I found myself as Director of the whole Newcastle Festival as a stopgap after the previous holder of the job left at short notice. My own tenure came to an abrupt halt when my 1970s ended quite literally with a bang. I crashed my motorbike and ended up in Intensive Care. But I still have fond memories of the decade.

Dick Godfrey

ncjMedia

Brian Gibson and Tom Hill of Geordie celebrate Brian's victory in the Radio One celebrities' charity race at Brand's Hatch; their clothing boutique Geordie's, next to La Capanella on Shakespeare Street, is in the background. Tom and his friends Brian, Vic Malcolm and Brian Johnson formed Geordie in 1972. Geordie took a final bow in 1977.

Oh you pretty things

It was dark in the seventies; you remember? The sixties had been bright and frivolous, with space enough for prancing. And then Hendrix died and the Beatles split up and the clouds gathered for the winter of discontent. Miners were belligerent, energy was in short supply; everyone had candles for when the lights went out, which happened quite a lot. We craved light and space and to compensate we walked around on platform shoes.

On one trip to London with my pal Pete Dowson, we infiltrated Kensington Market, shuffling around from stall to stall. Carnival. Music courtesy of Zappa, Marc Bolan, Joni Mitchell, Bowie, Sly and the Family Stone. There was nothing like this in Newcastle. The Handyside Arcade was diminished – with only Tony Jackson in the bookshop Ultima Thule, and the Kardbar to remind us of the good old days.

In Kensington we were seduced by a cornucopia of cheap stuff to buy, and I returned to Heaton with a waisted daffodil yellow zipped canvas jacket with a big floppy collar, hip hugging yellow loons, and blue suede high heeled boots with yellow diamond shaped appliqué up the sides. I loved those threads. When I was dressed I glowed. Those clothes enhanced me aerodynamically, the boots elevated me. I checked my reflection in the window of Jeavons' music shop with its Hofner and Epiphone guitars – heading for an assignation with the usual suspects in the Haymarket Hotel opposite the dirty angel. I grooved. I trucked like Mr Natural; so cool. My unruly khaki hair was back-combed and stood out from my head like a dandelion clock. There were two girls approaching wearing metallic hotpants, headbands, radical elevator shoes that eclipsed my blue suede boots. Hey, one of them called out, look at him (I didn't break stride), he looks just like a banana. They cackled, tottering precariously over the cobbles on their platforms. That was it, you see; we were ludicrous – we wanted to be.

Sean Figgis

And at the very very end ...

We were earning very decent salaries. Maggie Thatcher had just boosted the police by giving them huge pay rises, so in early 1979 we bought our own house. Each month we bought our food from Marks & Spencer – we budgeted £30 per month AND had money left over. Late on 31 December 1979 I gave birth to a gorgeous little girl. Despite being urged by the midwives to wait until 1980, she'd have to be happy with being the last child born in the 1970s. And that's when my life really began to change ...

Pam Wilson

High Bridge, 1970.

The contributors

Elswick Court, off Northumberland Street, between Fenwick and Finlay's, 1974.

Toon bands

Above, Sandgate, early 1970s.
Below, Junco Partners, around 1978.